NO REGRETS

Welsh Rugby's Plan To Conquer the World

'Matt has worked closely with the squad for the last few years. He has built up a trust with the players and coaches that works both ways.

Having that relationship doesn't remove his ability to be critical, it just means he is able to see and understand the bigger picture and what we are trying to do. It is the media's job to report and inform the public what is going on and having a respected relationship means Matt can do that from a position of knowledge and understanding.

Working with the media is not always smooth sailing but Matt is an honest, trustworthy journalist and I hope you enjoy the book and his account of the last few years!'

Warren Gatland

NO REGRETS

Welsh Rugby's Plan To Conquer the World

Matthew Southcombe

ST DAVID'S PRESS
Cardiff

Published in Wales by St. David's Press, an imprint of

Ashley Drake Publishing Ltd
PO Box 733
Cardiff
CF14 7ZY

www.st-davids-press.wales

First Impression – 2019

ISBN
Paperback: 978-1-902719-818

British Library Cataloguing-in-Publication Data.
A CIP catalogue for this book is available from the British Library.

Typeset by Prepress Plus, India (www.prepressplus.in)
Cover Design by the Welsh Books Council, Aberystwyth
Cover image © ZOPH/EFLO/PA Images

Contents

*To my parents, John and Susan, and girlfriend, Laura.
Without your unwavering support this book would
never have been started, let alone finished*

Acknowledgements

I have to start by thanking my publisher Ashley Drake of St David's Press. If nothing else, this project has taught me that publishing newspapers and publishing books are two vastly different things. Without your guidance, I'd have certainly got lost along the way.

It would also be remiss of me not to place on record my gratitude to my boss Paul Rowland, Editor-in-Chief of Media Wales, for allowing me to take on this project whilst on the ground in Japan. Many in his position would have resisted the idea but Paul was the opposite and trusted in me to do my job as a journalist before chipping away at the chapters in this book in what down-time I had.

Finally, to the players, coaches and entire backroom staff of the Wales national team, your co-operation and approachability meant it was a pleasure to deal with you amid some of the most highly-pressurised moments of your careers. I know journalists covering other nations did not enjoy the same level of co-operation. This is your story and I hope I've done it justice.

Matthew Southcombe
November 2019

Foreword

The 2019 Rugby World Cup was an unbelievable experience for me. Normally, as a pundit or a commentator, I would be following Wales during their campaigns but this time, as part of the host broadcasting team for World Rugby in Japan, I ended up commentating on 16 games and got to experience pretty much every corner of the country, moving around places like Osaka, Kumagaya, Tokyo and Yokohama.

I was commentating on teams like Samoa, Russia, Georgia, and Uruguay, teams who you wouldn't normally associate with the standout Hollywood clashes, but because I was getting to watch all of these different teams, I really felt like I was part of the competition as a whole and it was definitely the best World Cup I've ever been involved with, in any capacity. It was a phenomenal experience that will stay with me for the rest of my life. The way the tournament was put on, and the way the whole country bought into it was simply unbelievable.

Early in the competition, I commentated on Wales v Georgia for BBC 5 Live but a lot of the time I was in different parts of the country, observing as Warren Gatland's side were playing. To be totally honest, it's probably the first time since I retired in 2012 that I have just been able to sit down and watch a Welsh match on the television. Half of the production team I worked with were Welsh, so we always found a TV to watch the Wales games. I worked on Georgia's win over Uruguay in Kumagaya and then, in the press room, watched Wales beat Australia. It was also when we were in Kumagaya that we managed to find a random pub to watch the Fiji game.

It was all a bit random and pretty surreal at times but it was great to just watch the game almost as a fan. I say that, but all of Wales' big games in Japan were nerve-racking, they all went right down to the wire which made things slightly uncomfortable at times. The clashes against Australia, Fiji, France and South Africa were unbelievably tense and I was perched on the edge of my seat throughout, you couldn't relax for one minute. I suppose it was always going to be that way with Wales.

They flew out of the blocks against Georgia and played some amazing rugby in that first half. Naturally, I think they took their foot off the gas in the second half with one eye on Australia, and when I look at that win over Australia in Tokyo I just think that, emotionally, it took a lot out of the squad. For years, so much had been pinned on that specific game, there had been so much talk about how crucial it would be. Once the boys did the job there, at times it just looked a little bit like we were hanging on. Because that Australia game had been built up so much, it felt like Wales' pinnacle was that second game.

It is always difficult to go again when you win a game that has been hyped up as much as that one was. After that, we had to come from behind against Fiji and France and, eventually, injuries caught up and South Africa felt like a game too far. In many ways, though, the campaign epitomised Gatland's reign as Wales boss. It wasn't always pretty to watch but there is no way you could question the squad's heart and commitment. They gave everything they possibly could and, as a result, won games they probably should have lost.

Since my playing days the World Cup has only got bigger and the players are put under so much pressure during games. There is also travel to consider, the massive amount of media commitments, and the fact that players are usually in foreign countries that they don't understand. It's a logistical nightmare.

That all gets lost because fans back home only really see the 80 minutes on television. All that peripheral stuff is left in the shade. Unless you are a part of it, it's difficult to comprehend what goes into it.

Having followed Wales' every move over the last two years, few journalists are better-placed to chronicle the team's journey over that period of time than Matt. Wales ultimately fell agonisingly short in Japan but it was one hell of a ride, yet as this book shows, there is always a lot more that goes on at World Cups than meets the eye.

Martyn Williams
November 2019

1

The Three-Year Plan

"We knew we had to start doing things differently"
Martyn Phillips

The media were not kind: 'Humiliated in his own backyard' was the headline on the front of the *Western Mail* on Wednesday, June 16, 2016. The day before, Wales had been thrashed 40-7 by the Chiefs Super Rugby franchise in Waikato, Warren Gatland's hometown.

This was a homecoming that would live long in the memory for all the wrong reasons. It was a game sandwiched in between the first and second of three Tests against New Zealand and its relevance had been questioned far and wide. Was the extra game really necessary? Was it worth the added stress it would put on a squad that had already played a friendly against England before flying down to face the mighty All Blacks?

Those questions quickly turned to stinging criticism after a second string Wales side were convincingly beaten by a Chiefs team missing as many as 20 first-choice players and was made up of second- and third-choice options in some positions. It was the second time a team from this part of New Zealand had beaten Wales. The last time it happened, in 1988, Gatland was actually playing for Waikato – a side that would go on to also beat the British and Irish Lions in 1992. This time he found out what it was like to be on the wrong end of the scoreline.

On a damp night at Waikato Stadium, a Kristian Dacey try was the most Wales could muster in the face of a seven-try onslaught from their hosts. The set piece held, but Wales simply had no answer as they were cut to ribbons by players not even deemed good enough to feature regularly at Super Rugby level, let alone international level.

"It was disappointing in terms of morale. We were second best by a long way," said a mild-mannered Gatland after the match, but there was a sting in the tail as he added: "A number of players have been asking me personally about what they needed to do, wanting an opportunity and why they have not been selected for the Test team. After this performance there's some fairly simple answers." A stark message to those fringe players who had been banging on his door. It was a dark night. An embarrassing defeat.

By the time those *Western Mail* pages had arrived at the newsagents on the morning of June 16, a crisis meeting had already been held at a hotel in Wellington. A quiet, sombre flight had carried the squad and support staff from Hamilton to New Zealand's capital city of Wellington straight after the match, touching down in the early hours of the morning, to prepare for the second Test against the All Blacks.

After a few hours in bed, members of the Welsh management and Welsh Rugby Union hierarchy came together. They had already held a thorough review following the brave 2015 Rugby World Cup campaign, where Wales made it to the quarter-finals in England despite a staggering amount of injuries before and during the tournament. Led by Sam Warburton, they were eventually knocked out by South Africa, but less than a year after that review, the defeat to the Chiefs had forced them to reassess where they were going.

Head coach Warren Gatland, his trusted assistant Rob Howley, WRU chief executive Martyn Phillips and then-head of rugby performance Geraint John sat down at the team hotel to thrash out what would later be branded the 'No Regrets' plan. The meeting was robust and thorough, led by Gatland and Howley, as the four delved into what wasn't working and how they could rectify it.

There was no shouting and screaming. As he usually does, the Wales boss addressed the issues with calmness and pragmatism. A number of issues were identified but there were some particularly key problems to address: "We knew we had to start doing things differently, otherwise we were just going to keep getting the same results," said WRU CEO Phillips.

The biggest and most important shortcoming was that of depth. Gatland consistently brought up the word throughout the final few years of his Wales tenure. What the previous year's World Cup campaign had told him and his lieutenants was that Wales were short of multiple options in every position. They had a very formidable first XV that could challenge any team in the world, it had quality in every department. Gethin Jenkins, Alun Wyn Jones, Sam Warburton, Dan Biggar, Jamie Roberts, George North and Liam Williams were some of the stars. A strong spine, but beyond that starting side, what became apparent was that the depth chart simply wasn't deep enough. Wales always seemed to be an injury away from disaster.

A lack of strength in depth is something that will always undermine any World Cup challenge because, as Wales found out in 2015, injuries will happen, especially in a modern game where players are bigger and the collisions are more ferocious than ever before. The 2017 tour matches against Samoa and Tonga, when Wales' top management and players would be away with the British and Irish Lions in New Zealand, were identified as real opportunities to develop coaches as well as blooding new talent. In total, Wales contributed 12 players to that Lions trip, along with Gatland, Howley, skills coach Neil Jenkins, head analyst Rhodri Bown and national medical manager Prav Mathema.

It was just as important to develop the staff off the field as the ones who were on it. During that meeting in 2016, it was decided that regional coaches would be called upon for the Samoa trip in order to further their experience as well as contribute new ideas to the national setup. Nine players who went on that 2017 tour were named in Wales' final 31-man squad for the 2019 Rugby World Cup.

Also, even in 2016, it was decided that any players selected for the 2017 Lions would not tour Argentina in 2018 – although exceptions were made – giving them another opportunity to expose younger talent to the big stage. Wales could rely on the likes of Alun Wyn Jones, Dan Biggar and Jonathan Davies to step up when it really mattered, but they had to find out whether or not the likes of Elliot Dee, Adam Beard and Owen Watkin – all uncapped when the plan was hatched – could be ready in time for Japan. The theory was that if the new blood could provide them with a solid starting point, then when the Lions stars were re-integrated it would make them a fearsome outfit.

The second point of improvement was that they wanted to develop the senior player group and hand them more responsibility and influence moving forward. It was a team that already had respected individuals, but in the years that led up to the 2019 World Cup, a clear leadership group emerged and the individuals became more respected. In Japan, the leadership core included the likes of Alun Wyn Jones, Dan Biggar, Ken Owens, Jonathan Davies and George North. All those individuals were trusted to make decisions and set the perfect example both on and off the field. It wasn't all just on the captain.

More tactical points were also raised. The four in the room that day knew they were simply not clinical enough whenever they entered the opposition 22, another issue that needed to be addressed. They were also profoundly aware, perhaps because of what the All Blacks had shown in the first Test and continued to do so throughout the 2016 series, that the way the game was being played was changing. Wales' front five could no longer be content with a solid set piece, they had to become comfortable on the ball and link up with the back division in open play.

These were the key points that Wales had to address in the next three years. They had gone on that 2016 tour believing they could win the series against the All Blacks but had fallen well short. If Wales were going to be a factor at the 2019 Rugby World Cup, things had to change.

2

A Painful Relationship

"Judge me on the World Cup"
Gareth Jenkins

Wales have always had a painful relationship with the Rugby World Cup. It's either a brave defeat or an inglorious exit at the hands of teams they really ought to be beating.

The famous red jersey has been on display at every global gathering since the tournament's inception in 1987, and it's, perhaps, a tad ironic that the group which travelled down to New Zealand in the late 1980s managed to achieve what remains Wales' greatest ever finish at a World Cup.

Eight years before the dawn of professional rugby, those were very different times. Wales prepared for the tournament by spending a few days in Saundersfoot in Pembrokeshire, training at Tenby RFC before a 40-hour journey to Wellington.

The '87 World Cup, which didn't feature South Africa due to the international sports boycott against the *apartheid* state, was shared between Australia and New Zealand, with Tony Gray's side having the misfortune of playing their group matches in the latter. They would train in horrid conditions and then rush to get their kit dry for the following day's training session, all while watching games being played in baking hot conditions in Australia.

Back then, they flew in economy class, stayed in cheap motels and did their best to keep themselves occupied with table tennis and snooker tournaments. Cardiff great Mark Ring scored Wales' first ever try at a World Cup in the opening 13-6 victory over Ireland in a blustery Wellington. Winger Glenn Webbe chalked up a hat-trick, despite being concussed whilst dotting down his final try, in a convincing win over Tonga before Ieuan Evans scored four in a rout of Canada in a freezing Invercargill.

Then came the respite for Wales as they were finally sent to the warmth of Brisbane for a quarter-final match against England. They were too strong for the old enemy, winning 13-6 to set up a semi-final with the All Blacks when they were beaten emphatically by the eventual champions, who even back then were ahead of their time. A team featuring John Kirwan, Wayne Shelford, Sean Fitzpatrick, Michael Jones and Grant Fox were fitter, faster and stronger than all who came before them.

It was the game in which Wales lock Huw Richards was knocked clean out by one punch from Kiwi hardman Shelford yet, after he was brought around by the splash of a cold sponge, it was he who was shown a red card by referee Kerry Fitzgerald. Richards had dragged opposite number Gary Whetton out of a maul and landed a few punches of his own before Shelford landed his haymaker when the Welshman was looking the other way.

A fully amateur Wales side had no hope against a team featuring players who were already earning money appearing in adverts. They went down 49-6 but there was little shame in it. The Kiwis had scored 30 tries in just three pool matches and would go on to win the final against France convincingly.

Wales went back to New Zealand for their third place play-off against Australia, a game which they won in dramatic fashion.

With the crowd firmly behind them, Adrian Hadley scored a late try in the corner, which was converted by Paul Thorburn to secure a 22-21 victory. That third place finish has never been bettered by a Welsh side.

In the years before the next World Cup, an exodus of players to rugby league clubs in the north of England left Wales depleted. Stars like Paul Moriarty, John Devereux and, most notably, fly-half Jonathan Davies were among those lured away by the cash on offer. It meant Wales went into the 1991 edition of rugby union's showpiece event in bad shape.

They had finished bottom of the Five Nations in 1989, 1990 and 1991, winning just one game across the three tournaments and the Welsh Rugby Union dispensed with the services of then-head coach Ron Waldron in the summer of '91 after a 63-8 thrashing at the hands of the Wallabies.

New coach Alan Davies was given one game to prepare his side for that autumn's World Cup and it went as you might expect – miserably. The 45,000 who ventured to the National Stadium in Cardiff on October 6, 1991 witnessed one of the biggest upsets in World Cup history as Wales were humiliated by Western Samoa, losing their opening game 16-13.

Wales were not only left with their tail between their legs but they were battered and bruised. The visitors to Cardiff that day included the likes of Brian Lima – later nicknamed 'The Chiropractor' – Pat Lam, Frank Bunce and Apollo Perelini, and they left their mark.

Wales' Richie Collins and Phil May saw their World Cups ended by injuries as a result of crunching hits and Tony Clement was forced out of the next match.

Three days later, Wales would recover to a certain degree, beating lowly Argentina back in the Welsh capital. A try from Paul Arnold and the boot of Mark Ring did the damage but Wales' campaign would not become some glorious revival.

8

Just six days after that embarrassing defeat to Western Samoa – a sign of the times that they played three games in less than a week, which would never be allowed nowadays – Wales were dumped out of the tournament at the group stage by Australia. A Wallabies side that included the likes of David Campese, Michael Lynagh, Nick Farr-Jones and John Eales swatted Wales aside to the tune of 38-3 on their way to winning the whole tournament, beating the much-fancied All Blacks in the semi-final and England in the final.

The 1995 edition of the World Cup will live long in the memory because of the political climate that surrounded it. It was the first major sporting event to take place in South Africa following the end of *apartheid* and it was the first global gathering that the Springboks competed in. Not only did they compete, they went on to win the whole thing, beating New Zealand 15-12 after extra time in the final. Nelson Mandela, donning a Springbok cap and jersey, presented skipper Francois Pienaar with the trophy, producing one of the game's, and sport's, most iconic images.

For Wales, it was another World Cup to forget. Again, they saw a coach depart shortly before the tournament with Aussie Alec Evans hastily drafted in to become the first non-Welshman to coach the national rugby team. He took over eight weeks before the tournament in South Africa, a campaign that didn't last long.

Things started reasonably well with a convincing 57-10 victory over Japan, with a young Gareth Thomas scoring a hat-trick and Ieuan Evans crossing for two in Bloemfontein. However, that result was put in perspective later in the tournament when New Zealand put 145 points on the Japanese. Wales also, once again, felt the force of the All Blacks on the biggest stage just four days after their opening victory. Neil Jenkins' boot was the only source of points at Ellis Park in Johannesburg as the team went down 34-9 to the eventual runners-up. They still had a chance to make the knock-out stages but were narrowly beaten by Ireland in their final group game. Once again Wales left the competition far too early.

Two weeks after South Africa lifted the Webb Ellis Cup in their home tournament the game went professional, and the new era did lead to signs of improvement in Welsh rugby as the next World Cup approached, with Wales as hosts. A now infamous Welsh win at Wembley, with Scott Gibbs and Neil Jenkins combining to deny England the Grand Slam and the Five Nations Championship, came months before the 1999 World Cup as Graham 'The Great Redeemer' Henry's side became the first to get out of their World Cup group since the opening effort back in '87.

Enjoying all the home comforts as tournament hosts, Wales played all of their matches at the brand new cathedral of Welsh rugby, the Millennium Stadium. A seemingly favourable draw saw the team beat Argentina 23-18 in their opening game – Colin Charvis and Mark Taylor with the tries. Once again they thumped Japan, this time 64-15, before coming unstuck in embarrassing fashion, once again, against Samoa. Despite enjoying a dominant scrum that yielded two penalty tries on the day, Wales couldn't put the visitors to the sword, with the forwards in particular making countless errors.

Assuming a comfortable win, the Welsh supporters were mainly focused on Neil Jenkins becoming the highest points scorer in Test match history but the fly-half, who was usually punishingly accurate from the tee, missed kicks at goal and delivered a pass that was gladly intercepted by Samoa's Pat Lam, who ran the length to score a crucial try in the second half.

Jenkins eventually broke Michael Lynagh's record, making history in front of an ecstatic home crowd, but the Samoans well and truly rained on the parade, running out 38-31 victors in what was a thrilling match for the neutral.

"If we had won the game, and I had not scored a point, then I would have been delighted," Jenkins said at the time. "When the first kick I had hit the post, I thought 'here we go, it is going to be one of those days', which is something that can happen when you are a goal-kicker. When you concede 28 points from your mistakes, then you cannot hope not to be punished."

Despite that defeat, Graham Henry's side actually topped their group, edging out the Samoans with a superior points difference thanks to their demolition of Japan. However, their stay in the tournament didn't last much longer as they were knocked out in quarter-finals at the hands of eventual winners Australia, going down 24-9 in front of a packed Millennium Stadium. The Wallabies would return two weeks later to topple France in the final, putting the World Cup in John Eales' eager hands.

Wales were not widely fancied to leave much of a mark on the 2003 Rugby World Cup and, on paper, another quarter-final exit appears particularly unremarkable, but it doesn't begin to tell the whole story. They played their part in some incredible Test matches during that six weeks in Australia, with rip-roaring performances, albeit in defeat, against the All Blacks and eventual winners England.

Wales went into their opening game against Canada under immense pressure. By most metrics, Steve Hansen's side were too good for the Canucks but it was lost on nobody that this could easily prove to be a banana-skin game. They couldn't afford to slip up before they even got started.

After a tricky start, rugby league convert Iestyn Harris, who'd done little of note since making the switch to rugby union, played a starring role in the midfield, carving the Canadians up. His initial break set up the first of five tries on the night, scored by Sonny Parker. Gareth Cooper, Mark Jones, Colin Charvis and Gareth Thomas scored the others to run out convincing 41-10 winners, despite Charvis spending 10 minutes in the sin bin.

The team then stuttered and stumbled against Tonga seven days later in Canberra, though they didn't fall. It was far from an assured performance and, after Hansen rung the changes, it raised serious questions about whether or not they could get past Italy and take a step towards the knockout stages. Tries came from Gareth Cooper and Martyn Williams but the boot of Stephen Jones did the bulk of the work with four penalties and a conversion. It was also the game in which flanker Williams famously dropped a goal, helping Wales scrape through in a 27-20 win.

A strong defensive effort saw the team restrict Italy's scoring to five penalties in the third group match, with tries from Mark Jones, Sonny Parker and Dafydd Jones doing the bulk of the work in a 27-15 victory. There was little to write home about but Wales had achieved what had been expected of them and qualified for the knockout stages, though everybody thought the unbeaten run would end there. The only thing left to determine was the manner in which they exited the tournament.

However, ironically, Wales' most notable performances at the 2003 World Cup came in defeat. They faced the All Blacks in their final group game in front of 80,000 spectators in Sydney and they put on a real show. A glorious victory was always the stuff of fantasy but the performance warranted widespread praise.

Hansen decided to field a largely mix-and-match side to face a full strength All Blacks team. A cricket score was expected, but Wales boldly went toe-to-toe with the opposition and even outfoxed them at times with Stephen Jones, in particular, playing with a new air of confidence. Ultimately, the try-fest – there were 12 in all – ended in a 53-37 defeat, but Wales'

37 points was the most they'd ever scored against New Zealand, a record that still stands and it registered with England, who lay in wait in the quarter-finals.

What transpired in the quarter-final was almost unfathomable for many onlookers, as Wales rattled England to their very core. They made a mockery of the bookmakers and for periods, looked to be heading to the semi-final. Scores from Stephen Jones, Colin Charvis and Martyn Williams saw them outscore the old enemy three tries to one but it was the left foot of Jonny Wilkinson that destroyed Welsh dreams.

The game ended 28-17 and Clive Woodward's side would go on to win the whole thing but the performances against the All Blacks, and certainly England, sparked hope that Welsh rugby was now moving in the right direction. A nation was proud of their rugby team but dark times loomed.

When Mike Ruddock walked away from the Wales job in 2006, Gareth Jenkins was the only real candidate to take his place. His CV was impressive, despite being overlooked for the job in 2004, but it quickly became apparent that good club coaches didn't necessarily make good international ones. After a poor Six Nations, Wales' preparations for the 2007 World Cup didn't exactly go swimmingly either. A 62-5 thumping by England left many fearing for what might come in France. Boldly, Jenkins urged the Welsh rugby public to 'judge me on the World Cup' – a statement he would later regret.

The group stages initially went as expected as Wales opened their campaign with a comfortable 42-17 victory over Canada, helped along by a brace from Shane Williams and impressive kicking displays from Stephen Jones and James Hook. They also pummelled Japan, scoring 11 tries in all with wing Williams again scoring two along with his namesake Martyn.

Jenkins' side then lost their pool game to Australia 32-20 but there was no shock in that. The Wallabies were a considerable force, boasting the likes of George Gregan, Stirling Mortlock, Matt Giteau and George Smith to name a few. After that defeat, the 72-18 victory over Japan will have done the team's confidence the world of good but the storm clouds were gathering overhead as Wales faced a winner-takes-all match with Fiji in the final round of the pool stages.

The Pacific Islanders, though they were tricky opposition, were not supposed to cause Wales too many headaches and the men in red were fully expected to cruise into a quarter-final with South Africa. The Fijians had other ideas. Remarkably, against a side who thrive on open, running rugby, Wales threw caution to the wind and played them at their own game. They totally underestimated the quality of the Fijians and it turned out to be a day that would haunt those involved for the rest of their careers.

Flanker Martyn Williams looked like he'd put a rip-roaring game of rugby to bed when he crossed in the 73rd minute but there was still time for it all to come crumbling down. Fiji hooker Graham Dewes crossed with three minutes remaining, dumping Wales out of the World Cup in embarrassing fashion. After the match, Fijian players were approaching their Welsh counterparts for pictures and autographs. In reality, it should have been the other way around.

The WRU hierarchy had seen enough and within 24 hours of the final whistle, Jenkins was sacked. He travelled home from France with the squad, despite being relieved of his duties at the team hotel prior to departure. It was one of the most brutal, unceremonious sackings Welsh rugby has ever known but the WRU were adamant they would not be in that same position four years later.

3

Hope and Heartbreak

"We just feel that ultimately the result wasn't in our control"
Warren Gatland

The arrival of Warren Gatland as head coach brought immediate success in the 2008 Six Nations, but the next Rugby World Cup was still three years away. The Kiwi inherited a squad that was in transition and would require freshening up ahead of the global gathering in New Zealand. Wales ended up going into that tournament banking on a number of inexperienced players pulling it out of the bag, and they didn't disappoint.

Boldly, almost out of nowhere, Gatland made a 22-year-old Sam Warburton his captain for the tournament, leaving legend Martyn Williams out of his squad. A decision that also left Williams marooned on 99 caps, though he did claim his 100th a year later in a match against the Barbarians.

Heading into the tournament, fly-half Rhys Priestland had just four caps to his name, No.8 Taulupe Faletau had three, centre Jonathan Davies had a handful of starts and skipper Warburton had only 17 caps in total. But this was to be a tournament when that new generation of talent made names for themselves, along with the likes of Leigh Halfpenny and

George North. Dan Lydiate was also one that emerged in a tournament where his trademark chop tackle was introduced to the world.

Prior to the New Zealand trip, Gatland had revolutionised the way Wales prepared for big campaigns. He took the squad on camps to Spala in Poland, where they wrestled and trained on sand, under the watchful eye of highly-respected fitness guru Adam Beard, in a bid to become one of the fittest teams at the Rugby World Cup.

It was at those camps that Wales made using cryotherapy – where players enter a chamber and are subjected to temperatures of -120C – fashionable in professional rugby. This allowed the players to recover better and train harder, and more often, than ever before.

In the opening game against South Africa, Lydiate led the defensive effort, scything down the big Springbok runners and Wales almost, and maybe should have, caused a massive upset. They lost the game 17-16 but their exploits began to win over the hearts and minds of the Kiwi public. Wales became the locals' second favourite team behind the All Blacks.

Wales hadn't beaten South Africa since 1999 and the wait would have to go on, but controversy surrounded a James Hook penalty. Referee Wayne Barnes and his assistants Vinny Munroe and George Clancy deemed that it went wide. However, replays suggested it may have drifted inside the uprights and it would have made all the difference.

Regardless, Wales had made a statement in defeat and, despite there being no great expectation, would go on to be a real force in the tournament. Samoa proved to be stubborn but Wales eventually saw them off with a 17-10 victory before convincing routs of Namibia and Fiji. Centre Scott Williams ran in a hat-trick of tries against the former, with George North setting a record as the youngest ever try-scorer at Rugby World

Cup at the age of 19. The class of 2011 would avenge the embarrassment of 2007 with a resounding 66-0 thrashing of the Fijians, with Jamie Roberts charging over for two scores.

Wales sauntered into the quarter-finals where they faced familiar foes Ireland. The performance they produced that night in Wellington will go down as one of the greatest performances of the Gatland era. Skipper Warburton played some of the best rugby of his career, causing the Irish all manner of problems at the breakdown. George North was at his rampaging best, Jonathan Davies was irresistible and Mike Phillips was imperious. It was an emphatic 22-10 victory over Six Nations rivals and Wales charged into the semi-finals. Irish legend Brian O'Driscoll later called the defeat one of the biggest regrets of his career, but that was of no concern to Gatland's troops, who were on a roll and ready to do something special.

Over 60,000 turned up at the Millennium Stadium to watch events unfold on the other side of the world at Auckland's Eden Park. Wales were riding a wave of support – both at home and from the New Zealand public – and confidence as they strutted out to face France, but Gatland's world was flipped upside down when captain Warburton did the same to French winger Vincent Clerc in the 19th minute.

Expecting France to target him at the back of a lineout, Warburton was primed and ready for traffic to come down his channel and surely enough, Clerc came steaming towards him.

The openside lined him up immediately and hit him with everything he had. Warburton's superior bulk and strength saw him launch Clerc up into the air, letting him go in a panic as the tackle spiralled out of control.

Angry French forwards converged from all angles and referee Alain Rolland pulled out the red card so fast many missed it, including the Wales bench. When Warburton reached his spot on the touchline, having been sent off, skills coach Neil Jenkins gave him some words of encouragement and told him to keep warm, assuming he'd only been sin binned. The young flanker informed Jenkins of the colour of the card. The former fly-half was incredulous.

Despite that, Wales still had chances to win the game throughout. Mike Phillips went over with 23 minutes remaining on the clock to bring Wales to within a point but Stephen Jones missed the conversion. Leigh Halfpenny's late shot at glory from halfway fell devastatingly short and, despite a late onslaught, France held on to win by a point. It had never been so heartbreaking.

"I feel let down, I thought this team were good enough to go on and take the final but it was not to be. We just feel that ultimately the result wasn't in our control," fumed Gatland in the post-match press conference. "We just feel like the destiny of the result was taken out of our hands with the red card. He's lifted him, that's a yellow card, but he's not driven him into the ground. Does that mean every time there's a tackle where you lift someone off the ground it's a red card? Why spoil the semi-final with a red card? He's not a dirty player. I'm just gutted."

With the wind well and truly knocked out of their sails and their skipper banned, Wales fell 21-18 to Australia in the third-place play-off match and 1987 retained its title as Wales' greatest World Cup. In the final, New Zealand looked underwhelming as they stuttered to World Cup glory, beating France 8-7 and Wales was left pondering what might have been.

In the four years building up to the next World Cup, Gatland had turned his side into a real force in the game. They recovered from that 2011 disappointment by claiming a Six Nations Grand Slam in 2012 and another Championship in 2013. There was also a healthy Welsh contingent on the successful 2013 British and Irish Lions tour of Australia, in the coaching box and on the field. There was a slight dip in 2014 and 2015 with back-to-back third place finishes in the Six Nations, but there was a bigger picture and Gatland was beginning to prove that he could get teams to peak at just the right time.

Again the planning was meticulous. This time he took his squad to the altitude of the Swiss Alps for a camp, allowing the players to reap the benefits of that, with the theory being that when players recover at altitude, their body becomes more efficient at using oxygen. They then had a camp in the dogged humidity of Doha before finishing off their preparations back at their Vale Resort base just outside of Cardiff. The squad were due to have another camp in Poland, but that was binned with management taking the view that they had already made sufficient progress. Things had gone largely to plan, but disaster struck before the tournament had even begun.

In the final warm-up match against Italy, arguably Wales' best player in Rhys Webb and all-out points machine Leigh Halfpenny suffered devastating injuries. Webb, crying out in pain at the bottom of a ruck, could be heard 15 rows deep into the stand and, later in the game, Halfpenny slammed his headguard into the ground repeatedly – an uncharacteristic outburst of emotion – after twisting awkwardly. Both were stretchered from the field.

A horrible atmosphere descended over the stadium.

"Everyone knows it's been a bit of a disastrous day," said fly-half Dan Biggar after the game. "It was a massively disappointing and a tough afternoon with a couple of key injuries." When asked if it was a worst case scenario, Biggar added: "Yes it is. Just a couple of weeks before the tournament starts we have two injuries to two key players. It's disappointing and frustrating and we will have to see how they pull up before commenting further."

Gatland was heavily criticised for fielding such a strong side against relatively underwhelming opponents so close to the

World Cup. Both players would miss the tournament, but Wales had to plough on without them and they thumped Uruguay 54-9 in the opening Pool A match in Cardiff, with centre Cory Allen crossing for a hat-trick and Rhys Priestland kicking seven out of eight conversions.

Then, in six days, came one of the biggest games of the Gatland era: England at Twickenham in the World Cup. Stuart Lancaster's side will have felt like they were in control of the game for the most part but Dan Biggar – whose ability to fill the kicking boots of Halfpenny was doubted by many – kept Wales in the game with a series of penalties.

Heading into the final quarter, Wales trailed by four points but had lost Scott Williams, Hallam Amos and Liam Williams to various injuries. It resulted in replacement scrum-half Lloyd Williams ending up on the wing, and it was Williams whose break down the left and chip in field found fellow scrum-half Gareth Davies, who gathered brilliantly to slide over the line with nine minutes to go, making it 25-25 following an Owen Farrell penalty. Biggar then held his nerve to knock over another penalty from around halfway, booting Wales to victory on one of their most glorious nights.

A brutally short turnaround saw them face a bruising Fijian side just five days later, with Gatland's men slugging it out to win 23-13. It was a harsh test of their character and there were bodies strewn all over the pitch. After the emotional toil of beating England and the physical abuse dished out by Fiji, Wales were battered and bruised.

A frustrating loss to Australia followed but it mattered little, Wales were into the quarter-finals courtesy of the Wallabies already beating England, and dumping them out of their home World Cup.

Crippled by injuries – through the pool stage they lost Cory Allen, Scott Williams, Hallam Amos and Liam Williams – they came up agonisingly short in the quarter-finals as a late Fourie du Preez try saw them lose 23-19. They had fought admirably on the day – completing 177 tackles – to manufacture a winning position and keep South Africa out until the final five minutes but some brilliant skill from No.8 Duane Vermeulen saw him release the scuttling scrum-half down the blindside for a heartbreaking score.

"I couldn't have asked any more from the players in terms of the effort they have given," said Gatland in his press conference. "Wales can be very proud of these players and their performance, particularly to come out of that group which was so tough. You couldn't have asked for any more. They have given 100%. You saw that against the Springboks. They put their bodies on the line. They spent themselves and emptied the tank and that's the only thing we can ask for. So I am very proud of what they have delivered. Unfortunately we weren't good enough to hold on for 80 minutes."

The story of Wales at the World Cup has been one of self-inflicted, humiliating disasters or of glorious and heartbreaking defeat, but by the time they reached the World Cup in Japan, Warren Gatland's class of 2019 had already proven that they were different, that they were capable of rewriting history.

4

New Blood

"We don't feel we're a year or two years behind anyone else"
Warren Gatland

With a plan in place, all that was left was for Warren Gatland and his coaching staff to execute it. Creating a competition for places within the squad was top of the agenda and they simply had to blood new players, but there was a complicating factor.

In the 2015 Rugby World Cup, Wales found themselves in a 'Pool of death' with England, Australia, Fiji and Uruguay. This was because their official world ranking at the time of the draw, two years before the tournament, was so poor. They found themselves outside the top eight in the world, and third tier seeds, which meant a challenging Pool was inevitable.

Whilst the coaching team were keen to expose the next wave of talent coming through, they were also acutely aware that they simply could not find themselves in pot three when the draw took place in May 2017. As such, progress on the 'No Regrets' plan was slow. Between that New Zealand tour in 2016 and the trip to face Tonga and Samoa the following summer, just two new players were handed debuts. Lock Cory

Hill and fly-half Sam Davies both featured in a dismal 32-8 defeat to Australia in Cardiff.

There was frustration aplenty and the Wales hierarchy faced criticism from sections of the media who knew they needed to bring through new talent but were yet to see it. With Wales in a precarious position in the world rankings, the 2017 Six Nations would be pivotal to their chances and, to make things slightly tougher, they were without their head coach. Gatland had taken a sabbatical to concentrate his efforts on the impending British and Irish Lions tour of New Zealand that he would lead, leaving the task of securing at least eighth place in the rankings to assistant Rob Howley.

After rolling over for Australia, the 2016 autumn campaign went well, with wins over Argentina, Japan and South Africa and things were looking good with Wales fifth in the world after that campaign. However, defeat to England and then Scotland in the 2017 Six Nations meant those in charge were getting twitchy. Wales had slipped to seventh in the world and could ill-afford to slip much further. A 22-9 win over Ireland saw them jump to sixth but defeat to France on the final weekend saw them sink to eighth. They'd made it into the second pot by the skin on their teeth, and now it was time to focus on building a squad that could challenge at the 2019 global gathering.

With Howley assisting Gatland in New Zealand, the 2017 tour was led by forward coach Robin McBryde who was tasked with taking a closer look at certain players and figuring out the ones who could cut it. The intention was obviously to win every game, but results were not the ultimate goal: finding Test players was.

There were 11 debutants on that 2017 summer tour as Wales beat Tonga 24-6 at Eden Park in Auckland, and then Samoa in dreadful conditions in Apia a week later. Around 10 members of the squad were hit by a sickness bug on the day of the game but managed to grind out a 19-17 win thanks to second half scores from Steff Evans. The wins were almost a bonus but, crucially, a number of new players now had an understanding of what Test rugby was like, with five of those 11 debutants making it into Gatland's final 31-man squad for the Rugby World Cup – Wyn Jones, Ryan Elias, Dillon Lewis, Adam Beard and Aled Davies.

Before the 2017 autumn series, though, came news that left the jaws of most Welsh rugby observers on the floor. Wales' selection policy, dubbed 'Gatland's Law', much to the displeasure of the man himself, needed to be tweaked but the way it panned out left a strange taste in the mouth.

A new rule was being brought into effect immediately that stated if you had fewer than 60 caps and played outside of Wales, then you were ineligible for selection. Players currently in contracts outside of Wales, like Liam Williams at Saracens, were exempt, but Rhys Webb, who was on his way to Toulon after the completion of the 2017-18 season, was not.

There was uproar in Welsh rugby as the new policy left Gatland's first choice scrum-half – a Test Lion, no less – tantalisingly out of reach. Claim and counter-claim followed with the WRU suggesting he could wriggle out of the move having only signed a pre-agreement, but Webb's view was that he had to fulfil his commitment to Toulon and could not get out of the contract. Then there was an argument over whether Webb, who gave 11 years of service to the Ospreys, should be exempt given he had no knowledge that the law was coming, something that was then disputed by the WRU.

As the head coach, Gatland was always the face of the selection policies but he wasn't always the driving force behind them. In his ideal world, as national team head coach, he'd be able to pick whoever he wanted, regardless of where they played. "For me as a national coach, if I was being totally selfish then no I wouldn't have a policy," he said during the Webb saga. "But it's not about what's best for me and the national team, it's about what's best for Welsh rugby. The best thing for Welsh rugby and for the Union to support the regions is how do we try and keep a number of the best players in Wales for as long as we possibly can. But we know we're under pressure from market forces."

It was a messy affair and everyone lost out. Webb went to Toulon and was thus, by default, unavailable for the World Cup in Japan, stranded on 31 caps.

In November that year, Wales had a mixed campaign, with victories over Georgia and South Africa interspersed with more defeats to Australia and New Zealand. The result against the All Blacks was a particularly frustrating one for Welsh fans to stomach, having just contributed 12 players to the Lions squad which had drawn a series with the World Champions a few months earlier.

To make matters worse, Jonathan Davies, who was the star performer during that Lions series, saw his season ended in the final play of the defeat to Australia as he carried the ball into contact despite Wales being 29-21 down, with the clock in the red. He suffered a Lisfranc fracture and would be sidelined for 10 months. However, the No Regrets strategy saw another five players handed their international debuts during the campaign and three of them made it to Japan – Owen Watkin, Elliot Dee and Hadleigh Parkes, who scored on his debut against the Springboks.

After that Australia game, and what was deemed a fairly uninspiring autumn campaign, it was put to Gatland that his team were lagging behind England, Ireland and Scotland, and that the evolution of his squad should have begun much earlier. Prophetically, he staunchly rejected that criticism. "The game is not about changing it's about evolving. We don't feel we're a year or two years behind anyone else," he said. Gatland and his coaches had a plan, and they were sticking to it.

The Six Nations is not the place to breed new talent and so there was just one debutant in the 2018 campaign: Josh Adams, whose stunning try-scoring exploits for Worcester Warriors meant Gatland simply couldn't ignore him. He was raw, though, and made a costly error in the England game at Twickenham when he was caught way out of position as Owen Farrell kicked in-behind for Jonny May to score.

Wales were defeated in London and flat-out bullied by Ireland in Dublin a fortnight later. That was a difficult day at the Aviva Stadium. Whatever you say about Wales under Gatland, particularly in the second half of his tenure, they were stubborn and difficult to break down. Defence coach Shaun Edwards deserves the credit for that, but Ireland had their way with them and there will have been plenty of soul-searching on that flight back over the Irish Sea.

Closing wins over Italy and then France repaired some of the damage but little did anyone know Wales were now on their way to creating history. For that 38-14 victory over Italy was the first of the historic 14-game unbeaten run, the longest in Welsh rugby history.

A real statement was made on the 2018 summer tour to Argentina, via a game in the USA against the Springboks, as Gatland left 10 of the 2017 Welsh Lions at home, only taking George North (hamstring) and Ross Moriarty (back), both of whom had suffered injuries on the Lions tour. It was a tour where new leaders would emerge and young talent would be nourished. The trip was not about results. Gatland never openly admitted it – how could he? What sort of message would that send? – but it went better than he could have ever imagined.

An opening game against a weakened South Africa side in Washington was heavily criticised. Players didn't need the extra Test at the end of a long season, said some. Former Wales international Gwyn Jones described the game as a 'shambles' and Gatland fired back, labelling the critics 'bitter and twisted'. Whatever your view, an inexperienced side, led by one of the tour's co-captains Ellis Jenkins, ground out a 22-20 victory in damp, muggy conditions. Scrum-half Tomos Williams, making his debut, scored a try and setup Ryan Elias' winning score with a charge down in the closing stages.

Wales went on to steamroll Argentina in a two-Test series, enjoying a 23-10 victory in San Juan and a 30-12 win in Santa Fe. It was supposed to be an intimidating atmosphere but a new-look Wales side walked in with a swagger. They silenced the crowd early in both games, stretching out to leads in the opening quarters. They would go on to close both games out comfortably.

Flanker Jenkins, who captained Wales imperiously in the opening game against the Springboks was then dropped from the 23 for the game in San Juan. It was a decision that turned heads but it was symbolic of Gatland's plan. He was headstrong. It didn't matter that Jenkins had played well, they had to take a look at James Davies and this was their chance.

Harsh on Jenkins? Probably, but there was a much bigger picture here.

Gatland consistently chopped and changed his 23 throughout that three-Test trip and continually came up trumps. Even with a very inexperienced group, Wales were undefeated and there was plenty to be optimistic about. After the first victory in South America, Gatland was asked if the performance will give him a headache when it came to picking his team the following week: "I think the boys sat at home watching on the TV have probably got a worse headache than I have," he grinned as his plan came together. Then, after the clean sweep was confirmed a week later, he told the small travelling press pack: "Sometimes in smaller nations you get comfortable and complacent — that happens when you don't have a huge amount of depth. What's pleasing is that now we've created something where there isn't any complacency.

"There are so many players at the moment that have helped create depth, and players know that when they take the field it could be their last opportunity in a Welsh jersey and they'll want to make the most of it. That, to me, is the most pleasing aspect of this tour. We've now got a group of guys sitting at home who now realise their positions aren't guaranteed. They're going to have to work hard. The players that have been on this tour have really put their hands up."

Scrum-half Williams and back-rowers James Davies and Aaron Wainwright all made their debuts on the trip – all three made the final 31-man squad for Japan – and Gatland would head into the 2018-19 season with the strongest Wales squad he'd ever had at his disposal. After what he described as the most pleasing tour of his Wales tenure there was suddenly competition for every position, but his bubble was about to be punctured.

Out of the blue, two-time Lions captain Sam Warburton, the man Gatland installed as Wales skipper at the age of just 22, announced his shock retirement from the game on July 18, 2018. After leading the Lions in New Zealand, Warburton missed the entire 2017-18 season, undergoing neck and knee surgery in a bid to get fit for the World Cup year. "Unfortunately after a long period of rest and rehabilitation the decision to retire from rugby has been made with my health and wellbeing as a priority," Warburton said. "My body is unable to give me back what I had hoped for on my return to training."

Warburton, one of the most likeable men in the game, had been through the mill. His list of injuries and operations was astonishing and alarming in equal measure. Years of fearlessly putting his country before his health had caught up with him.

He had reported for pre-season with the Cardiff Blues with every intention of reclaiming his Wales jersey in time for the World Cup the following year, but the decision came about quickly.

So quickly, in fact, that there wasn't so much of a whisper in rugby circles that it was even coming. For a story of that magnitude to stay under wraps, it must have progressed at speed.

It was a huge blow for Wales. One of Gatland's favourites, a talisman of his tenure, had gone, but the wheels had to keep turning. In October 2018, Gatland summoned in excess of 60 players to the team's headquarters at the Vale Resort: classic Gatland. It was a move that told every player in attendance that they were in consideration for the World Cup squad. It sharpened their focus and served as motivation for them to make sure they were the best professional they could be.

That month the Kiwi named a 37-man squad for the autumn campaign, during which Wales began a habit of warming up before matches with a squad of 31 players on the pitch. This replicated a Rugby World Cup environment, which permitted the larger number to be involved before matches to ensure the starting XV had effective opposition during warm-ups, and illustrated the coaching team's meticulous preparations for Japan 2019.

Again, the WRU came in for criticism when they arranged a game outside the designated World Rugby international window against Scotland in Cardiff. It was said to have devalued the fixture but, in hindsight, those at the top of the organisation insist it was vital. Wales hadn't beaten Australia for a decade and they usually faced the Wallabies early in the autumn campaign. Wales were notoriously slow-starters in international blocks and it fed the doubt that had crept in.

Having been drawn in the same Pool as the Wallabies in the World Cup, everyone accepted that Wales had to beat them before the tournament itself purely to give players the belief that it was possible. They went on to sneak past Australia 9-6, and there are some at the WRU who believe that might not have happened had they not played Scotland, and beaten them, a week earlier. The value of that win over Michael Cheika's side cannot be overstated.

Wales went on to enjoy another successful campaign as a 74-24 rout of Tonga and a 20-11 win over South Africa followed. It was now nine wins in a row, but it came at a cost. Flanker Ellis Jenkins, who had excelled at Test level since making his debut on the 2016 New Zealand tour, suffered a horror knee injury. It was a cruel blow as he'd established himself as one of the premier opensides in Wales and been particularly outstanding in that win over South Africa. It was an injury that would rule him out of the World Cup, that was still 10 months away.

Three players made their debuts in that campaign – Jarrod Evans, Jonah Holmes and Luke Morgan – though none of them made the World Cup. It was also a campaign where Gareth Anscombe really came of age on the international stage and wrestled control of the No.10 jersey from stalwart Dan Biggar. The Cardiff Blues pivot would start the 2019 Six Nations in possession of the No.10 shirt on a sodden night in Paris.

Gatland bullishly claimed that if they beat France then it set them up to win the Championship but things could hardly have gone worse for Wales. Tries from Louis Picamoles and Yoann Huget gave the hosts a 16-0 lead at half time in the Stade de France. All the positive energy surrounding the Wales squad that had been built up over the past year seemed to have deserted them, but a double from George North and a score from Tomos Williams put them, remarkably, in the lead, with Biggar coming off the bench to kick his goals and help steer Wales to a dramatic victory.

Again, to replicate a World Cup scenario, Gatland's side didn't return home from Paris. Instead they had a mini-camp in Nice before heading to Rome to face Italy. Biggar was rewarded with a start and a chance to reinstate himself as Wales' premier fly-half, but it didn't go to plan for him as he appeared too keen to impress and perhaps forced things.

Neither outside half had nailed down the jersey after being handed opportunities and it was becoming a problem. Nonetheless, Gatland's side made it two from two despite making 10 changes to the side that had beaten France.

Anscombe got the nod at No. 10 for the crunch game against England in Cardiff as Gatland hit upon the perfect formula. England were on top in the first half but in the second there was only ever going to be one winner as tries from Cory Hill and Josh Adams sent the Principality Stadium into the stratosphere. It was also Wales' 12th straight victory – a new record. Perhaps more importantly, though, Anscombe began dovetailing very nicely with Biggar, with the latter's pragmatism proving to be exactly what was required to see tight games out.

Away from the Six Nations, Welsh rugby spiralled into chaos the week of the Scotland game as a proposed merger between the Ospreys and Scarlets collapsed. It was a terrible week for the players, with many unsure whether they had a contract for next season, or where they'd be playing. The players were forced to interrupt their tournament preparations and travel to their regions for emergency meetings on days off. The whole affair was incredibly unsettling, but they managed to grind out an 18-11 victory at Murrayfield in what was a very physical encounter. Players left the field bloodied, battered and bruised but the job was done.

For the final weekend of the championship campaign, Ireland boss Joe Schmidt insisted that the roof at the Principality Stadium be kept open, despite the damp forecast, assuming it would favour his side. How wrong he was. The game never looked in doubt as Wales controlled from start to finish. Confidence oozed from the team as they raced into a 16-0 half time lead thanks to an early Hadleigh Parkes try and the boot of Anscombe.

North was forced off the field after just eight minutes, suffering a fracture in his hand, leading to a backline reshuffle with Biggar coming on, but this side had now proven they could handle adversity. More Anscombe penalties followed and the game was sealed in the second half. Ireland were never in it. Jordan Larmour scored a try at the death to ensure Ireland didn't have to leave Cardiff scoreless, but the 25-7 win was emphatic.

It was the third Grand Slam of the Gatland era and Wales would head into the Rugby World Cup as the northern hemisphere's premier side: Six Nations champions. Expectation levels had never been higher.

5

No Stone Left Unturned

"It's good enough to win (the World Cup)*"*
Warren Gatland

On April 30, 2019 Warren Gatland named a 42-man Rugby World Cup training squad. It was slightly more trim than many were anticipating and there were some casualties. The most high-profile omissions were those of Dan Lydiate and, particularly, Jamie Roberts. They had been two stalwarts of the Gatland era and, in many ways, players around which the gameplan had been built for years.

Lydiate had struggled with injuries in the season leading up to the squad announcement, featuring just nine times for the Ospreys. Roberts had been playing regularly for Bath but Hadleigh Parkes had taken to international rugby perfectly and had a telepathic relationship with Jonathan Davies, his Scarlets team-mate. Since Parkes' debut, Roberts hadn't played for Wales.

With player welfare such an important part of the modern game, the players reported for the pre-World Cup camp at different times. There was a staggered return as every player was given four weeks off from the end of their domestic season.

They were sent away to totally switch off from the game, to rest and relax ahead of the what was going to be a tough three months of training.

The Dragons' season finished on Judgement Day at the end of the Guinness PRO14 season, so all Dragons players arrived in camp on May 27. There were just six of them at this point. Cardiff Blues players were due in camp on June 10, bumping the numbers up to 13. Their season ended on the same day as the Dragons but the region continued training as normal as there was a chance they were going to make the Champions Cup play-off.

In the end, the Scarlets ended up playing the Ospreys in that play-off match, meaning the bulk of the squad, including Worcester's Josh Adams, didn't arrive until June 17. Up until this date it had been a sort of mini-camp. Players were just ticking over and doing work to ensure their fitness levels didn't drop off too much. Many questioned why it was necessary to have certain players in so early, but the fear was that if the Dragons players, for example, were given an extended break away from training, then they would suffer a significant drop off in fitness ahead of the real work beginning. That would only make the task harder when it came to really whipping the squad into shape.

When the cavalry had arrived, the real work could start. Dan Biggar, Tomas Francis and Liam Williams all arrived slightly late, after featuring in the Gallagher Premiership play-offs. Having already won the Six Nations and the Champions Cup, Williams capped a remarkable season by clinching the Premiership with Saracens before arriving in Wales camp.

Wales' preparations would see them take in a fortnight in the Swiss Alps and a week in the blistering Turkish heat. In 2015, the squad had reaped the benefits of training at altitude in the sleepy Swiss village of Fiesch. Once again, the squad operated a 'live high, train low' policy that saw them spend around 20 hours a day at their chalets high up in the mountains, over 2,000 metres above sea level.

They would then come down the mountain in gondolas to around 1,000 metres above sea level to train on a local football ground, with rugby posts erected at one end. As soon as training was over, they'd head straight back up the mountain to recover. The theory is that your body becomes more efficient at using oxygen because there is less of it available. Then, when you are back down to around sea level, you can recover faster.

"I remember the first night I was up there trying to get to sleep and my heart was beating a lot harder than normal, which is unusual," said flanker Aaron Shingler. "You get up for the toilet in the night and you have to climb a little bit of stairs and your heart is beating (fast) again. It just feels like you're working when you're sleeping."

Sections of the media were invited to observe two days of training at Fiesch, a stunning little village nestled into the Alps, with a raging river bisecting it, but there was nothing beautiful about what the players were being put through, it was pure, unadulterated graft. There was nothing fancy about what was going on. Players were continually asked to push themselves to the limit, but it was all done in a safe environment and they were carefully monitored via all the various data available to the analysts, with staff on hand and ready to pull any player from a session if he was pushing it too hard.

That fortnight in Fiesch was unforgiving but it was more successful than four years previously. Back then, all they did was fitness but in 2019, the players were so much fitter that they were able to introduce more rugby sessions and skills work earlier in the programme.

"To be honest, this camp has been better than last time. We've got through more work," said the larger-than-life Paul Stridgeon, the WRU's head of physical performance at the time. "The boys are coping with the workload better. We're really happy with it. When the boys came back in, some of them actually had personal bests, beating their scores from four years ago, and that was before we started the camp. So, to be fair to the boys and the regions, you can see they've worked hard and we started off in a much better place than last time."

Gruelling sessions would really test the players' skills under fatigue. They would play variations of touch rugby designed to work them aerobically, then it would be straight into a power endurance circuit and then onto some skills work, for example. Rarely did sessions run over an hour and then of course there was a weights programme to complete as well. It was tough, but they were preparing to become the best team in the world.

After a solid camp in Switzerland came the first injury blow. Taulupe Faletau had played only once since October 2018 after fracturing his arm on two separate occasions but was finally on the mend. He looked short of fitness in Switzerland but the signs were promising as he began taking contact. However, during a session back at the Vale, he carried into contact, just like he would every other session, and ended up breaking his collarbone and requiring surgery. His World Cup was over before it began. Losing the two-time Lion was a hammer blow, but Wales had coped without him during their unbeaten run.

Then the warm-up matches began and the schedule was, once again, heavily criticised. Four warm-up matches, home and away, against top opposition in England and Ireland felt excessive. It felt as though the WRU were playing with fire, especially in light of the injuries they suffered in the warm-ups four years ago.

Prior to the first game against England at Twickenham, I put the criticism to Gatland and he candidly admitted: "The criticism (of the schedule) is fair. You can't get it right all the time. You are trying to negotiate warm-up games with sides and trying to get the balance right. I think the England games are always a good contest for us. You may have wanted three [games], or potentially not quite so strong opposition, but you go into negotiations, and sometimes you have got to accept what has been delivered. I understand exactly where you are coming from, and I understand the criticism as well. That's warranted. It's a little bit of a concern that you don't pick up too many injuries, but sometimes you have just got to roll the dice and go with it."

Gatland went full strength for back-to-back matches against England on August 11 and 17. A bold move that raised eyebrows, but it replicated the six-day turnaround that Wales would have between Georgia and Australia at the World Cup and the players needed to experience it. Wales were well beaten 33-19 at Twickenham first up, but there was no major cause for concern as the majority of their problems could be chalked up to rustiness. Outside the camp there was concern, but in it there was calm.

The scrum needed urgent attention but Wales created a number of chances that were thwarted by misplaced or dropped passes. The real worry, though, was an injury that Gareth Anscombe sustained. He had become Wales' top fly-half and was looking increasingly assured in the No.10 jersey with every passing game. His role looked nailed on as a starter, leaving it to Dan Biggar to come on and finish the job. Anscombe tried to play through the pain after falling awkwardly early in the first half but was eventually replaced by Biggar in the 34th minute.

Scans later revealed damage to his anterior cruciate ligament. It was another Welshman's World Cup over before it began, and it was heartbreak for a player who looked poised to really set the tournament alight. From Gatland's point of view, he'd lost a major weapon in his arsenal.

Anscombe, distraught as he obviously was, still found the time to post a message on Instagram after the news broke: "Not quite the way I was hoping my World Cup dream would finish. Been a pretty tough 24 hours to take but I'm very thankful and humbled for all the kind well wishes. Still wrapping my head around what's happened and what's next but I'm excited to watch this Wales team go on and do something special."

Wales were far better a week later when England visited Cardiff. The intensity was back in their defence and it was much more of what we'd come to expect from Wales. In the build-up to the match, Biggar came under fire from rugby legend JJ Williams, who insisted Wales couldn't win the World Cup with him at fly-half. The Northampton Saint produced a man-of-the-match performance as he orchestrated the 13-6 victory, before thanking Williams for providing him with the perfect motivation in a post-match television interview.

After the match, Williams' comments about Biggar were put to Gatland and he jumped to the defence of his player, firing back at Williams in the process: "He [Biggar] needed to play at 10 because he's been coming off the bench and we've been starting with Anscombe," explained Gatland. "I thought he was really good today. I don't know about that former Welsh player. Was he really old? Did he play in the '70s? Did he play 50 years ago? Probably. That does explain a few things."

Gatland and Biggar were criticised for their comments but I thought it was all pretty fair. As a journalist, I am never going to castigate somebody for speaking their mind. I had no problem with Williams' comments and no issue with Gatland and Biggar firing back. Everyone has a right to get something off their chest, particularly the person being criticised in such fashion, and I would take no issue with anyone challenging my opinions. It keeps things interesting. Gatland and Biggar did nothing out of order.

It was also a victory that saw Wales officially move to No.1 in the rugby world rankings for the first time in their history. Wales were then whisked off to Turkey for a heat camp before returning to Cardiff to welcome Ireland.

Details of the heat camp were slightly thin on the ground and no media access was granted during that trip. What we do know is that they went to Turkey in an attempt to replicate the hot and humid conditions players were going to have to battle against in Japan. From what players have said since, it was every bit as gruelling as the fortnight in Switzerland.

Gatland and Ireland boss Joe Schmidt had agreed to name experimental sides in the first game of the double-header before picking a strong XV for the return fixture in Dublin. It was the last and, for some, the only chance to impress. Rhys Carre and Owen Lane made their debuts in the match but all eyes were on the fly-halves. Jarrod Evans and Rhys Patchell were both given 40 minutes to prove their worth, fighting it out to be Biggar's deputy in Japan with Gatland deciding he only wanted to take two fly-halves.

The Cardiff Blues pivot started the game but he spent the entire half on the back foot and made mistakes that ultimately did for his chances. By contrast, Patchell looked confident, pulled the strings nicely and almost hauled Wales back into the match with a try in the second half. Wales lost 22-17 but their biggest conundrum had been answered. Patchell would go to the World Cup and Evans would not. Some felt this was unfair on Evans. I wasn't in that category. It was utterly brutal, I concede that, but at the end of the day this is professional sport and at times it is a cut-throat business. The injury to Anscombe meant Gatland didn't have long to decide which of his back-up fly-halves were up to the task. It was tough on Evans but, if it was a straight shootout, there was only one winner and it was Patchell.

The following day, Gatland named his final 31-man squad for the Rugby World Cup and, true to form, had kept some big decisions up his sleeve. There was utter shock and genuine disbelief when Rob Evans, who had played in 11 of Wales' 14 games unbeaten, was nowhere to be seen. You would have been forgiven for thinking that the WRU had dropped a clanger on their press release. Samson Lee was also absent. Surely something was amiss.

"When we decided to go with the five props, one of the big discussion points was how durable they are," explained Gatland. "Rob hasn't trained a lot in the lead up to the warm-up matches. He came in with a shoulder injury, then he's picked a neck injury and a couple of back issues. Rob hadn't played a lot. Samson has missed a few campaigns through injury, had a hamstring issue during the campaign. We looked at the durability of the props coming in. Someone like Rhys Carre has made incredible progress. He's dropped 10kgs, thought he did well yesterday, he's a big man. Apart from one day, where his calves were a bit tight, he hasn't missed a training session or been in the physio room. All the other props are also pretty durable. That was probably some of the consideration that we had in taking five props."

As he spoke, Gatland's big call began to make sense. Lee had taken very little part in every open training session that the media were allowed to attend and, if Evans was carrying niggles, could Wales really take him to the other side of the world?

Another interesting omission was that of the experienced Scott Williams. The Ospreys centre has played at two World Cups and appeared to be back to full fitness after a season plagued by hamstring and back problems, but it was later revealed that the fact he even featured in the game against Ireland was an incredible achievement as, when he first arrived in camp, his back issues were that bad he'd struggled to bend over to pick up a ball.

It was also made public that Cory Hill – who hadn't played since scoring in the victory over England in the Six Nations – was carrying an injury that was worse than the Wales management had previously let on. He was instructed to spend the week travelling back and forth to an oxygen chamber in Swansea to aid his recovery, and that his World Cup hopes were still in the balance.

Whatever had gone before, Gatland was confident: "I think it's good enough to win [the World Cup]," the Kiwi said of his squad." The most difficult thing about this squad is the depth we've created over the last three or four years, so we've left out some real quality players. In the past when you've picked a World Cup squad, you may have been happy with 24 or 25 players and the others making up the numbers, you're not sure about their quality, but this time we've left out some class players. I thought Owen Lane played well yesterday and is definitely a player for the future. We've left out two experienced props and Bradley Davies, an experienced player, has been left out as well. Then you've got players who aren't available, someone like Rhys Webb, so the depth of the squad and the difficult decisions we've made is a sign of the preparation that's gone into the last three or four years. So I think we go there with a lot of belief and self-confidence."

Wales were beaten again, 19-10 in Dublin, this time with a strong side out, but, in light of what had happened four years ago, the most important piece of news was that there were no serious injuries. Patchell failed a head injury assessment (HIA) after a thunderous collision with CJ Stander but he would recover in time to make the plane.

I sensed a fair bit of trepidation around Wales and among my fellow journalists as the team rounded off their warm-up schedule. On the face of it, the results were not pretty, not by any stretch, but I thought the worry and criticism was slightly premature. I'd watched players look rusty and make mistakes they don't normally make. Wales blew four or five good chances against England at Twickenham, for example. That was never going to transpire in Japan and, with all due respect, Georgia was the perfect opener because they would provide some form of opposition but should ultimately not cause too many issues. The warm-ups had not made me more confident in Wales' chances, but they had not made me less so either.

The preparation was done and it was time to head to Japan. On September 11, Warren Gatland all his support staff and all 31 players boarded a flight from Heathrow to Tokyo, or so we thought.

6

The Dream Becomes a Nightmare

*"You have to deal with adversity at times, and it's how you
respond and react to that."*
Warren Gatland

It's Tuesday, September 17. The clock is ticking towards 10pm.
My laptop is still warm, having just filed my final piece of copy
for the day – Mike Phillips' first column of the World Cup for
WalesOnline. A text comes through alerting the small pack of
journalists that have followed Wales to Kitakyushu, that an
announcement is due at 1am Japan time. Very unusual.

It didn't take long for me to receive a message from a source
to say that Rob Howley has been sent home from Japan, before
laying out a series of allegations. It couldn't be true... Could it?

When handling stories like this, there are a series of laws
that prevent journalists from simply running any old rumour
about somebody. If you get it wrong, there's every chance you'll
be facing a lawsuit for defamation. One source simply wasn't
enough to run the story that this person was telling me. What
became apparent when I was trying to stand the story up was

that very few people knew exactly what had gone on. Even the players were kept in the dark until very late on.

Eventually the story broke in the *Daily Mail* and the WRU put out the following statement:

> *"The WRU can confirm that Rob Howley has returned to Wales to assist with an investigation in relation to a potential breach of World Rugby regulation 6, specifically betting on rugby union.*
>
> *The decision was taken to act immediately in light of recent information passed to the WRU.*
>
> *No further details can be provided at this stage as this would prejudice the investigation. If required an independent panel will be appointed to hear the case.*
>
> *Rob has co-operated fully with our initial discussions and we would ask that the media appreciate this is a difficult and personal matter for Rob and that his privacy is respected before an outcome is reached.*
>
> *Warren Gatland has consulted with senior players and Stephen Jones will be arriving in Japan imminently to link up with the squad as attack coach."*

The tip-off that had stopped me in my tracks was true. Wales attack coach Rob Howley had been relieved of his duties and sent home from the World Cup before it had even begun after he found himself at the centre of investigation into an alleged breach of World Rugby's betting regulations. The immediate reaction was utter shock. This was scandalous, it was unthinkable. The gravity of the allegations simply took a while to sink in.

Having dealt with the initial breaking story, it was now 2am and time to get some sleep. After a quick phone call to Mike Phillips to tinker with his column – suffice to say the news agenda had changed – it was time to try and switch off.

The next day, the WRU handled the crisis admirably and a clear timeline of events emerged.

The Union were contacted on Wednesday, September 11 – the day the squad flew out to Japan – by the integrity division of a betting company. Proceedings were informal at that stage as the betting company moved to verify that Howley actually was the person concerned.

That approach then became formal on Friday, September 13 as more information was presented to the WRU. It prompted CEO Martyn Phillips and head of rugby operations Julie Paterson to fly out to Kitakyushu, where Wales were basing themselves, to confront Howley. They arrived on Monday September 16 – by now, the management team were aware of the allegations – and immediately sought two separate meetings with Howley, during the day, to present him with the evidence that had been provided by the betting company. At that point, Howley was sent home.

That Monday, Wales received an astonishing welcome by the locals. Over 15,000 filled the local stadium to watch them in an open training session. It was a remarkable occasion. The session was sandwiched between Howley's meetings with Phillips and Paterson but he was present at the Mikuni World Stadium. It was an occasion that will live long in the memory of those who were there but it was tainted for Gatland and his management team because they knew what was about to unfold.

That day, the Wales boss met with a number of senior players – the likes of Dan Biggar, Alun Wyn Jones and Jonathan Davies – to break the news to them. They then had to decide who would be called up to replace Howley. Stephen Jones, who was due to take over from Howley after the World Cup as part of Wayne Pivac's coaching staff, was Gatland's first choice but he was not forced on the players. The players agreed with the boss: Jones was a popular choice, having played with or coached the majority of the squad.

The next day, team manager Alan Phillips went to a team managers meeting in Tokyo, where people from other countries were all talking about the phenomenal reception Wales had received in Kitakyushu, but Phillips too knew what was coming.

On Tuesday, September 17, the rest of the players were informed and then the news broke to the public. Rather than hide behind their brief statement, the WRU met the crisis head on. Phillips and Gatland held a press conference on Wednesday, September 18, during which the CEO provided information on what the investigation would entail.

Gatland was probed more on how the news affected the squad and the emotional side of things. Howley was one of Gatland's most trusted lieutenants. Their relationship stretched back two decades, to when Howley played under Gatland at London Wasps. The former scrum-half had been a mainstay on Gatland's coaching staff throughout his tenure as Wales boss and he had no idea. Nobody had any idea.

It was a chain of events that shook Gatland and the entire group to its core. In that press conference, Gatland slumped in his chair while Phillips had the look of a man who'd just flown around the world at short notice and was in the midst of managing a crisis. It was not easy for anyone in that room, least of all the two in front of the cameras. After years of planning, this was supposed to be a glorious swansong for Gatland and his assistants as the majority of them were due to move on following the conclusion of the World Cup. With just days before the first game, he been blindsided by this, but he still had to prepare the side to face Georgia.

"We were shocked," a crestfallen Gatland said at that press conference. "The Union are dealing with this, and my focus has to be on the next five days in terms of preparing the squad for the first game against Georgia. I spoke to Stephen Jones the other night about his availability, and he was willing to help.

He has either played or worked with two thirds of the squad. He will bring his own personality and have the opportunity to have his input and his own ideas. That's important. For us, it is to make it as seamless as we possibly can. You have to deal with adversity at times, and it's how you respond and react to that. This has happened. I must say that the players in the last 24 hours have really stepped up and they have been incredibly responsible and resilient, and sometimes that brings teams closer together. We have got to draw a line in the sand on this, and really focus on preparing the team for the next five days."

Jones wasn't due to link up with the squad until they arrived in Toyota City to face Georgia, in the meantime, senior figures Dan Biggar and Jonathan Davies stepped up to take more responsibility in training. The tangible impact Howley's departure had on the side never appeared to be that great. Here were a group of players – including many British and Irish Lions stars – who had been together a long time. After months of preparation, they were on auto-pilot.

"It's not the ideal situation but we've just rolled our sleeves up and got on with it", said Biggar. "We still have to go out on Monday night and try and deliver a result. It was pretty disappointing. For people like myself, all we've ever had is Rob as a coach in this set-up. He's given us every cap we've had, but we're also adults and realise that we have to just try and get on with it and that's what's been great about this squad. Whatever has come our way, we're strong."

Another theme throughout the press conference was that of concern for Howley's wellbeing. Phillips was keen to stress that, whatever he was alleged to have done, Howley remained an employee of the WRU and as such the organisation had a duty of care to him. When Howley returned to the UK, a number of national newspapers attempted to seek him out in his hometown, though it was rumoured at the time that he never returned to his home and instead sought shelter in a holiday cottage.

"It's very hard to do something about something you don't know about," said Phillips. "I am pleased in the way we and World Rugby have reacted – what we are seeing is rugby taking the allegation seriously. I don't feel personally a form of embarrassment around that. It was a serious allegation about Rob. He's our employee and we have a duty of care to him and his welfare is important to us."

Social media became awash with wild speculation and rumour as to what Howley actually did. Most of it seemed like nonsense and trying to dig out exactly what was being alleged was nigh on impossible with so few people actually in the know. At the time of publishing this book, it is still only alleged that Howley contravened World Rugby's betting policy, and an investigation will be carried out. It is not yet confirmed exactly what Howley is alleged to have done.

It was an unfortunate and frantic start to Wales' World Cup campaign that overshadowed the phenomenal welcome the team received in Kitakyushu. A team from the WRU, headed up by former internationals Rhys Williams (business development manager) and Ryan Jones (performance director), had been running a legacy programme in the city for the 18 previous months along with a number of community coaches and regional managers. They had made countless trips there to deliver coaching clinics, hold mass participation events and grow the game in the area. The end game was to 'turn Kitakyushu red' in time for the players' arrival.

Local emergency service vehicles had Welsh flags painted on them, buses were covered in Welsh rugby branding, the local Kokura train station had huge posters of the players all over it and Welsh flags hung from the rafters, while Kokura Castle was illuminated red. When the players touched down at the local airport, hundreds of fans came to greet them.

I'd spoken to a lot of people and written stories myself about the work that had gone on in Kitakyushu but, deep down, you can never be sure whether the hearts and minds of the locals have actually been penetrated. When I saw youngsters turning up at the airport to welcome the team, I knew something special had been created.

Players spent time taking pictures and signing autographs. One moment stood out for me as I overheard Dan Biggar saying "arigatou" – thank you, in Japanese – after he signed every autograph and posed for every picture. This is the sort of thing that often gets overlooked but I thought it spoke volumes about Biggar himself and the values instilled in the squad.

Kitakyushu really was going crazy for Wales and it was impressive to see, especially given the sport wasn't hugely popular in Japan before the tournament arrived. On my first afternoon in Japan, one of the locals mistook me for one of the players. After a few minutes of trying to explain that I was a writer, the chap finally understood, I hope. By the time I'd finished my coffee, two more people approached me. It was surreal.

Then came the open training session. WRU staff were confident that they were going to pull off something special but there always seemed to be that little bit of doubt. Just how many people would actually turn up?

The answer was over 15,000 as they packed out the local stadium. Welsh hymns and *Hen Wlad Fy Nhadau* were sung by locals before the players went through a typical session in the baking heat. It was a genuinely spine-tingling experience and it was stunning to see that the locals had made the effort to learn the songs. In fact, on their first night in Kitakyushu, a welcome dinner was put on for the squad by local dignitaries and school children sang the Welsh hymn *Calon Lan*. That is usually Wales' go-to hymn but they quickly had to change their plans because the children had sung it better than the players. In the end, they went with *Lawr Ar Lan y Môr*.

Afterwards, they spent time signing autographs and taking pictures with the locals, something they did at every opportunity through the entire trip. After that open session, there was the welcome ceremony, which Howley didn't attend, and a few more training days before the tournament began.

What almost got lost that week was that Wales were one man down. Second row Adam Beard was not present with the rest of the squad. The talented lock, who had created some real competition for the place alongside skipper Alun Wyn Jones, was nowhere to be seen.

I learned about this very soon after landing in Japan myself. At the time I was the only journalist in Kitakyushu and the squad hadn't even arrived. The second row was still in the UK, I was told. Furthermore, he was in hospital. Eventually the WRU issued a statement confirming that Beard had not flown out to Japan with the rest of his squad after having his appendix removed in an emergency operation.

That first week of the trip was supposed to be relatively low-key. It turned into the most frenetic few days of the entire tour. Wales travelled up, by bullet train, to Toyota City, where they would face Georgia in their opening pool match. After the enormous welcome they'd received, Wales' dream start to life in Japan had turned into a nightmare and suddenly Toyota City looked very enticing. Questions about Howley and Stephen Jones persisted for a while but now that there was finally some rugby to talk about, the saga began to fade away.

"If I am brutally honest, I wish we were playing tomorrow. I can't wait to get going," said Neil Jenkins, who played with

Howley for many years. "It is obviously very difficult. He [Howley] is a very close friend of mine. It's not ideal, but it is what it is. It's happened, and we have to move forward. I have spoken to Rob. He was okay. I don't want to say any more. It is pretty private as far as I am concerned."

Ken Owens added: "It's been difficult. It's been a bit of a shell shock to the boys, We haven't had time to reflect or dwell too much on it because we have got a job to do. Harsh as it sounds, that's what we're here to do and that's what the focus has been for the last two years."

Shortly after the squad arrived in Toyota City, lock Beard joined them. He'd arrived at the team hotel hoping to avoid the players but it was horribly timed. The coach was parked outside with all the players on it ready to go to training when Beard arrived at the hotel.

He was late on tour, he'd lost weight and he was wearing the wrong kit for travelling. They amounted to three separate fines and it was not a great start to his trip.

We later learned exactly what his personal ordeal had entailed but more on that later. Gatland had always planned to go all guns blazing for the first three matches. Georgia were tricky opponents but if Wales were credible challengers for the trophy, they'd have to brush their opening opponents aside. Based on the noises coming out of the camp, both on and off the record, the Georgians were in for it.

Up until this point, I hadn't really seen a Welsh fan in Japan. I'd seen plenty of locals supporting Wales but nobody from back home. Toyota City wasn't the most attractive stop on the trip and many fans only arrived the night before the game and left shortly after.

Wales' team hotel was right next to the Toyotashi station, which most of the fans would use because it was the nearest to the stadium. It was a straight road to the stadium from the station and it was lined with pubs. As such, most fans ended up congregating in these establishments around the Wales hotel.

On the day of the game, I bumped into Wales' press officer amongst the crowds as I left the train station and headed to the ground. He told me he'd been listening to Wales fans singing hymns outside the pubs whilst taking his morning shower. No doubt other members of the travelling party and possibly the players will have heard the same. I was in no rush so I headed for the main drag and hung around for a while. It felt like home. Everywhere you looked there was red. *Hymns and Arias, Calon Lan* - they were all being belted out.

I'd been told by tournament organisers previously that around 15,000 Welsh fans were making the trip, though that was a very rough estimate. It was great to see so many Welsh fans enjoying themselves and it was clear the squad would be well-supported.

Wales were one of the last teams to kick off their campaign and, after all the Howley stuff, the players were desperate to get onto the field. It showed. It was the most razor sharp attacking performance Wales had produced for a long time. Well, for the first 40 minutes anyway.

Right at the end of Wales' warm-up, right in the final 45 seconds, there was a moment of concern. Dan Biggar and James Davies, who was not playing that day, clashed heads in one of the final drills. The fly-half stayed down, before ignoring some final hits on the tackle bags and heading straight down the tunnel with a medic. I was ready for the worst when the teams emerged. Fortunately, from Wales' perspective, Biggar was present. We later learned that he'd required stitches in those moments just before the players came out for the anthems.

Jonathan Davies tore through a gaping hole in the Georgian defence to get things going in the second minute. In celebrating that try, there was more woe for Biggar. The fly-half was congratulating Davies when Liam Williams arrived on the scene a little too excitedly and clashed heads with Biggar, who took another painful blow to the face just minutes after having stitches. These were not dangerous, concussive blows, simply the annoying whacks that are distinctly uncomfortable, but two clashes of heads within minutes of each other was not ideal for Wales' first choice fly-half.

Wales were targeting a weakness at the back of Georgia's lineout and Josh Adams breezed through a gap there on two separate occasions. The first time it led to a Justin Tipuric try and the second time he finished it for himself. Gatland's side were utterly rampant as Liam Williams got the bonus point score before half time, giving Wales a 29-0 lead at the break.

We saw some new stuff from Wales in that first half and it gave me real hope that Gatland had been keeping some tricks up his sleeve. They had clearly game planned masterfully to take advantage of some poor defence at the back of the Georgian lineout, where Adams twice took inside passes from Dan Biggar. We also saw one instance where Ken Owens wrapped around a lineout and fired a pass into midfield, with Gareth Davies providing some misdirection.

For Liam Williams' try, we saw Wales tweak their familiar attacking shape. Usually, if a forward is about to carry, he will be flanked on either side by a team-mate. Wales regularly pass to the first forward, who will then either carry or shift it quickly to the man next to him.

On this occasion, though, they threw it out the back to scrum-half Davies, who had come on the wrap-around and found acres of space, straightening up beautifully to glide through and send Wales on their way.

The second half was a slightly different story as the Georgians, who looked like rabbits in the headlights in the opening half, finally turned up. They became far more stubborn and got two tries of their own, much to defence coach Shaun Edwards' disappointment. Replacement Tomos Williams went over for one and George North rounded the night off with a well-deserved try of his own after a brilliant offload from scrum-half Williams. It ended 43-14.

Wales had taken their foot off the gas, it was clear they already had one eye on Australia, but the way they'd put the game to bed showed that they meant business. It wasn't so much that they had beaten Georgia, but after everything that had happened the manner in which they'd dismantled their opposition proved they were legitimate contenders.

In the aftermath of the win, there were some queuing up to praise the immediate impact of Stephen Jones on the Wales attack. That was misplaced. He'd had minimal influence on the way Wales approached that match. He'd only been in camp a matter of days before the game was played and the game plan had been mapped out months ago.

It was Howley who deserved the credit for the way Wales attacked that night in Toyota City and after the match Gatland admitted it was "strange" not having him in the coaches box, but it was job done and next up were Australia. It was time to move to Tokyo.

"We've been watching the games in the last few days and the guys were itching to get out there and I am pleased with the first-half performance," said Gatland. "I thought we were pretty clinical and probably let things slip a bit in the second-half. That probably did not help because we were losing some continuity and making some changes with the subs and bringing people off, trying to think about keeping players as fresh as we possibly can with the six-day turnaround. I think we can take a lot of confidence from that, they're a tough side."

From this point onwards the Howley saga began to drift away. While it would be in the squad's best interests that the

Wales' 2015 Rugby World Cup campaign started brightly with a thumping 54-9 win over Uruguay, followed by a famous 25-28 victory against hosts, England, at Twickenham. (© Shutterstock)

A disappointing 15-6 defeat to Australia hinted at what was to come, and Wales' World Cup dream was ended in a 23-19 quarter-final loss to South Africa. (© Shutterstock)

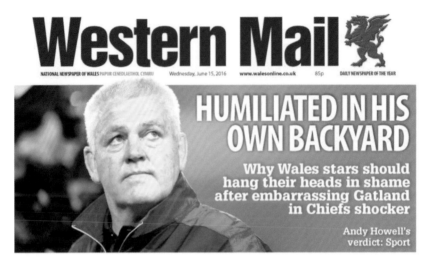

The 40-7 humiliation in Hamilton during the 2016 summer tour to New Zealand led Warren Gatland and his coaching team to rethink their strategy and devise a new plan: No Regrets. (© MediaWales)

Gatland's plan suffered a major blow in July 2018 when his inspirational captain Sam Warburton was forced to retire from rugby due to injury. (© Shutterstock)

Many fans questioned the point of the 2018 autumn international against Scotland, but it was viewed as necessary preparation and set Wales up to beat Australia the following week. (© Shutterstock)

2019 was arguably Gatland's most successful year. He guided Wales to another Six Nations Grand Slam (the third under his management) and a record-breaking 14-game unbeaten run which, in August 2019, saw Wales ranked as World Rugby's #1 team. (© MediaWales)

Full of confidence, the Wales squad headed to picturesque Fiesch in Switzerland for their World Cup training camp. (© Author)

The camp was gruelling but the players still managed to enjoy the breathtaking views. (Left: © Elliot Dee, Right: © Author)

Wales played four warm-up games during the late summer. A 33-19 loss to England at Twickenham was reversed with a 13-6 victory in Cardiff. There then followed two disappointing losses, home and away, to Ireland: 17-22 and 19-10. (© Shutterstock)

Wales blow as Faletau forced out of World Cup

TUESDAY, AUGUST 13, 2019   WalesOnline.co.uk

The end of the world as Anscombe is ruled out

The training camps and the warm-up games saw significant injuries to key players Taulupe Falatau and Gareth Anscombe which ruled them out of the World Cup. (© Media Wales)

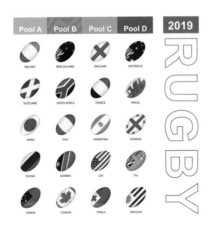

The squad arrived in Japan full of hope and the expectation of reaching the latter stages. The people of Japan were waiting. (© Shutterstock)

The crowds that came to meet the team at the airport were friendly, excited and numerous. Wales were big news. (© Author)

Over 15,000 local people thronged to the open training session at Kitakyushu and serenaded a stunned Wales squad with a perfect rendition of *Hen Wlad fy Nhadau*. (© Author)

At Lake Biwa in Ōtsu, the players enjoyed the reception laid on for them by local dignitaries but were completely oblivious to the massive storm raging overhead. (© Author)

Jones flies out as Wales hit by shock Howley exit

A storm of a different type engulfed the squad when attack coach Robert Howley was unexpectedly sent home and replaced by former international Stephen Jones. (Above: © Media Wales, Below: © Author)

At the official welcoming ceremony the players received their special World Cup caps and entertained the assembled guests by singing *Lawr Ar Lan y Môr*. (© Author)

Despite the shock of losing their long-standing attack coach, the players focused on the task ahead of them, and still found time to relax. (Left: © Josh Adams, Right: © Tomas Francis)

During a break from their pre-match preparations, Alun Wyn Jones and Ken Owens visited a local school with forwards coach Robin McBryde where they experienced another warm Japanese welcome. (© Author)

The final warm-up before the games in Japan would have been familiar to the Wales players and coaches. The squad had been warming-up with 31 players – as allowed in the Rugby World Cup and in preference to the standard 23-man squad – since the 2018 autumn internationals. This was all part of the No Regrets strategy. (© Author)

Wales eased to a 43-14 win over Georgia. A decent start to the tournament. (© PA Images)

In between the games, the players were clearly enjoying each other's company and the humour was infectious. (Left: © Josh Navidi, Right: © Hadleigh Parkes)

Wales v Australia at the Ajinomoto Stadium, Tokyo. The key game of the group. Unlike in 2015, Wales were victorious 25-29, were almost through to the quarter-finals, and on the preferred side of the draw. (© Author)

Full of confidence, the Wales fans travelled to the Showa Denko Dome in Ōita for the game against Fiji. Surely the disaster of 2007 in Nantes wouldn't repeat itself, would it? Wales won 29-17 but it was far from convincing and the bruising encounter had a severe impact on the squad. (Above: © Shutterstock, Below: © PA Images)

A straightforward 35-15 victory over Uruguay saw Wales through to the quarter-finals. The No Regrets plan was on course and the players could enjoy some time with their families. (© Leigh Halfpenny)

Another red card in a World Cup match between Wales and France, this time against French forward Sébastien Vahaamahina, gave Wales the momentum to win a game where they had been second best. A try from Ross Moriarty in the closing minutes secured a last-gasp victory, much to the delight and relief of the Welsh players. (© PA Images)

A tale of two kicks in Yokohama. A rushed dropped-goal attempt by Rhys Patchell saw an opportunity to take the lead lost while, 90 seconds later, Handre Pollard took the Springboks three points ahead with five minutes remaining. An exhausted Wales team couldn't respond and the 2019 World Cup campaign ended in the despair of another semi-final defeat. (© Media Wales)

The magnificent Wales fans took the defeat on the chin and stayed in Japan to support the team the following weekend in the third-place play-off against the All Blacks. (© Shutterstock)

A severely depleted and battered Wales gave everything but were outplayed in a 17-40 defeat to a superior New Zealand team. As the All Blacks celebrated with their departing coach Steve Hansen, the Wales team bowed in thanks and respect to their fans and the Japanese people. (© Author)

South Africa were crowned Rugby World Cup champions and celebrated in front of their own fans back in Cape Town. Will Wales ever enjoy a moment like this? (© Shutterstock)

The No Regrets strategy took Wales to a Grand Slam, a 14-game unbeaten run, a period as World #1 and a narrow World Cup semi-final defeat. The players gave their all and many will still be at their peak in 2023. What strategy will the Wales coaches devise for the next Rugby World Cup in France? (© Shutterstock)

WRU conduct their investigation as quickly and thoroughly as possible to draw a line under it, the way in which Wales won and the size of the game that was coming in Tokyo six days later meant the news agenda moved on and away from Howley. The storm had passed.

7

Overcoming The Aussies

"I'm very fortunate that I have a supportive wife!"
Stephen Jones

I'm fortunate to have done a fair bit of travelling in my time, following the Welsh rugby team for much of it, but I have never been more disorientated than when I arrived at Tokyo's Shinjuku Station.

Thousands upon thousands of commuters squeeze through the ticket gates there every day, and standing still in the sea of people is probably more dangerous than moving – even if you're going in the wrong direction. Don't hang about, just find a way out, and when you eventually locate one of the exits that takes you to the street, a neon glow from the countless shops, bars, cafes and restaurants stuns your eyes. Chatter, traffic and music fill your ears. This was like landing on another planet. I've never experienced anything like it. Welcome to Tokyo.

Wales had arrived to take on the Wallabies but there was bad news to deal with first. Cory Hill's World Cup was over. He wasn't able to recover from the stress fracture in his leg as quickly as the management team would like and, with Adam Beard already struggling for fitness, rather than carry him any longer, the decision was made to send him home. It was tough on Hill. He'd worked his socks off to try and regain his fitness and take part in the tournament but it wasn't to be. Not only that, in the last few years he'd emerged as a really important cog in the machine, another leader in the side in many ways. He was very highly-rated and his loss was a big blow.

The happy-go-lucky Bradley Davies was called up. Not only is Davies a good character to have in your group when spending so much time away, he's also vastly-experienced, having played at two previous World Cups. He seemed the natural choice but there were question marks over what he had left to offer at this level.

Upon the team's arrival in Tokyo, it was time for attack coach Stephen Jones' first press conference. Such are the media requirements placed on teams, every coach meets the media once-a-week. Jones couldn't be hidden away any longer and it was time to hear his thoughts.

Of course, the first thing on the agenda was the whirlwind week that saw him called out to Japan at such short notice in the midst of the Rob Howley saga. He should have been on the school run back home. Instead he was at the New Otani Hotel in Tokyo, speaking to gathered journalists.

"When I got the call, it was a straightaway decision," he said. "I'm very fortunate that I have a supportive wife as well! It was an instant decision. It's been manic, if I am honest, but what a wonderful welcome I have had from the boys and the management. I have worked with a number of the players and management before. The senior players were excellent - they took the helm and took the lead - which was great. Obviously, there is a wonderful foundation in place. There are a lot of good things in the library already. Gats has been excellent and said I can evolve things slowly, but obviously I am conscious there is going to be limited grass time, but where I am fortunate is that there are so many good things in place."

The former fly-half isn't a character who is ever likely to give too much away but, from the outside looking in, his appointment seemed like the logical one. He was due to take over from Howley after the World Cup anyway and was familiar with pretty much everyone in the camp already. He would also benefit hugely from seeing how the regime under Gatland operated before joing Wayne Pivac's coaching staff after the tournament. It certainly seemed like Wales had made the best of a bad situation.

The New Otani Hotel, where Wales based themselves in Tokyo, is a stunning and vast complex - the players were cutting it fine to make their first press conference as it took them over 10 minutes to walk from one side of the complex to the other - covering a land area of 69,226m², with 1,500 rooms and a Japanese garden, complete with waterfall. The huge structure comprises three different buildings that house a shopping arcade, coffee shop, a Bentley and Rolls-Royce car garage, outdoor swimming pool, tennis courts, spa, hair salon and just about anything else you could imagine. Life was good in the Wales camp. They were staying in a stunning hotel and just quietly going about their business. The Australia team hotel should have been a happy place to be as well. They were staying just a stone's throw away from Tokyo Disneyland, out in Tokyo Bay, but a storm was brewing.

Winger Reece Hodge had been handed a three-match ban for an illegal tackle on Fiji's Peceli Yato during the Wallabies' opening 39-21 victory, but that was just the start of it. The documents containing the full published decision gave details of the disciplinary hearing, including personal accounts from the people involved. It didn't make great reading from an Australian point of view.

Hodge admitted that he had no real understanding of World Rugby's new tackle framework and hadn't been trained to adhere to it. This was alarming because player safety is now paramount as the sport battles to reduce the number of concussions that players are suffering, and the framework had been given so much publicity heading into the tournament. Everyone knew officials would be punishing high or illegal tackles harshly. The report read: "The player (Hodge) conceded that he had no effective knowledge of World Rugby's 'Decision making framework for high tackles'; had not been trained on it; was not across it because the tackles he makes are predominantly in the waist to knees area."

The admission didn't go down well, especially in light of the fact that teams were given briefings on the framework before the tournament began. Yato's account of the incident itself made for grim reading as well. "From the moment he hit my face I blacked out and woke up when I was on my back," said the Fijian flanker.

In the week of such a big Test match, this is the kind of talking point that you want to nip in the bud. Letting it drag on all week creates a distraction but, remarkably, the Wallabies fanned the flames. It was a PR nightmare. A furious Michael Cheika, the Aussie's head coach, kicked off his press conference before a question was even asked.

"I wanted to say something at the start about some chat around the framework not being spoken to (by Australia) to the players," he said. "It came out in the judgement, the judge put that bit in there. I want to make a couple of points: the framework is for referees, not the players, to decide whether there are red or yellow cards in a game. The officials are using that framework very well in matches. Our players are coached to tackle in the middle. We do not need the framework to tell them how to tackle. I am not sure where that is coming from. We are not teaching anyone to tackle other than the middle where they can dislodge the ball."

This controversy was still rumbling on just 48 hours before the crunch Pool D match with Wales. On the other side of town, Gatland must have been rubbing his hands together with delight. The vibe around the Wales camp could not have been more different. Gatland had his big guns fit heading into the biggest game of the tournament. They were staying out of the headlines, keeping their counsel and going about their business with a quiet confidence.

It was cool, calm and unflustered. If you had to ponder which camp you would have rather been in, it wouldn't have taken you long. There was a steeliness to Wales, an edge.

On the day the teams were announced there was a feeling that they were going to beat Australia. They made all the right noises and revealed there was an edge to training. Blood was spilled and Ross Moriarty was in the thick of it. He'd failed to regain his place in the starting XV from youngster Aaron Wainwright, who just five years earlier had been in Cardiff City Football Club's academy. The Dragon was now starting a crunch World Cup clash and Moriarty had to be content with sitting on the bench, like a caged animal.

"Those sessions have been quite tasty and Ross has been at the forefront, leading them," said Wainwright, totally unflustered by the situation in which he found himself. "He's disappointed at missing out but, fair play to him, he has given everything in training. He has been really good in that sense." Wainwright carried himself remarkably throughout the entire tour. He had come from nowhere over the last two years and was suddenly playing in huge games at a World Cup. He seemed totally unfazed by the whole thing.

On the day the team was announced, Gatland and Jones sat next to each other on a top table at the press conference, where the coach confirmed that his captain would once again keep his place in the second row and become Wales' record cap holder with 130 appearances. Jones is a man who is distinctly uncomfortable with praise and it became apparent in Japan that he hated the Wales coach being asked questions that required a response which praised him.

Before the Australia game, the Kiwi was asked a question by a journalist who was essentially looking for Gatland to eulogise about the man sat next to him. Recalling that before the Georgia game, when Jones equalled the caps record, Gatland had been asked a similar question, Jones jumped in: "You did that last week, don't do it again!" He joked, but Gatland ignored the pleas and went on to praise the skipper regardless, adding "We don't have as many fights at training anymore because he used to start most of them. That's how competitive he is."

Jones sat next to him with a straight face. At the end of his gushing praise Gatland turned to him and said: "Was that okay?" His skipper responded: "I'll pay you later." Wales couldn't have been more relaxed.

Meanwhile, bizarrely, on the eve of the match, Wallabies boss Cheika met the media to fire yet more shots at World Rugby and his critics over the Reece Hodge saga. The Aussies just couldn't let it go and they just kept stirring the pot. Cheika rubbed a lot of people up the wrong way and, granted, I didn't have too many dealings with him but I actually enjoyed his press conferences. I had absolutely no idea what he was going to say next, which kept things interesting: "We've deliberated with our QC [Queen's Counsel] and several other legal minds around Australia and we have come to the conclusion we won't be appealing," said Cheika. "If they can't see that tackle doesn't meet the red card threshold on first view, I worry a little bit about going back there and getting more. From the moment he was cited, we sat down as a group and said it's not going to distract us from what we need to do." From the outside, though, it looked like that's exactly what was happening.

A lot was made of this match but I never really bought into the hype of it as much as many. Yes, it cannot be ignored that Wales beating a side like Australia would provide them with a confidence that should launch them deep into this competition, but there was no jeopardy to the game. The loser of the match would not be out of the World Cup and the setback would only be minor. The biggest inconvenience would be that they'd end up in the trickier half of the draw for the knockout stages. It wasn't an all-or-nothing sort of match but it was still Wales' biggest of the Pool stage.

When I got to the ground, it was clear that the Wales fans were outnumbered, with huge pockets of yellow all over the stadium. It didn't feel like a neutral venue, it felt like Wales were playing away from home.

I learned many years ago to take the emotion out of it when it came to covering the Wales team. It should come as no surprise to anyone that I was a fan growing up, but I've had to strip all that away. It's quite sad in some ways but otherwise it would be impossible to do my job effectively. That said, the anthem still gets me sometimes.

That evening in Tokyo, as *Hen Wlad Fy Nhadau* was being belted out by the fans and the players, it was very emotional and, as a Welshman, I definitely found it spine tingling. Naturally, it was quieter than it is in Cardiff but there was something in it that really struck me. Alun Wyn Jones has spoken in the past of the way the anthem connects the players to the fans before matches. For some reason, I really sensed that on this occasion.

When the game kicked off on a warm, sweaty Tokyo evening, it became clear that this was a different Wales. Inside the first minute, Dan Biggar was back in the pocket to slot a drop goal. It was the sort of tactical nous that this group of players had acquired over the years. It was an ability to execute and manage occasions in the face of significant pressure. This side was different to the ones that had gone before it and that drop goal, though it was only worth three points, illustrated it.

Wales dominated the opening exchanges and Hadleigh Parkes' converted try gave them a deserved 10-0 lead. The Wallabies hit back through a contentious Adam Ashley-Cooper try – there was a hint of crossing in the build-up – then came a big moment in the match.

Samu Kerevi was charging down the near touchline and looked destined to score. Biggar came from nowhere to throw himself into the path of the rampaging 108kg centre, halting him and saving a try. His bravery was commendable but his technique was not. He'd put his head in exactly the wrong position and paid the price. He was taken from the field around the half hour mark for a head injury assessment after being left sprawled out on the turf. Rhys Patchell came on. Biggar never returned.

It was the ultimate Test for Patchell, who himself had suffered four concussions in the last two years and there were significant question marks over his defence. This was the biggest challenge of his career but he was up to the task. Bernard Foley dragged the Wallabies to within two points but Patchell's first meaningful contributions were to bang over two penalties to re-establish a little buffer.

Then came a controversial moment when Kerevi charged at Patchell with a raised forearm that came dangerously close to his throat, resulting in a penalty. The controversy was compounded when Aussie skipper Michael Hooper slammed Patchell's tackle technique as he contested the decision with the referee: "Should we not run into the tackle there?" Hooper said to Romain Poite. "That's just terrible tackle technique and you can't carry the ball if that's going to be the ruling."

I thought a penalty was a good call from Poite. Hooper let himself down with the way he approached the referee and I thought the French official should have told him as much.

Regardless of Patchell's technique, you are taught from a young age that you are not to run into contact with your elbow raised. I didn't think it was dangerous enough to warrant a card in this instance but it had to be a penalty.

Hooper was making Patchell out to be the offender when everything the fly-half did was well within the laws. In fact, Shaun Edwards later explained that Patchell was doing exactly what he was told, he'd been encouraged to tackle a little higher than he had been and 'create the collision'.

Shortly afterwards, scrum-half Gareth Davies provided a defining moment of the match when he flew out of the defensive line – a trademark of his – to intercept a Will Genia pass and score. Davies had been shooting out of the defensive line for some time. We saw him do it regularly in the 2019 Six Nations – getting in the face of an opposition fly-half. This time, though, he'd picked the pass out perfectly.

Biggar had returned to the bench after failing his HIA to watch the rest of the match. The fly-half has his critics but the man loves Wales and he loves rugby. He is the ultimate competitor, and lived every pass, tackle and kick throughout the rest of the game. At half time, Biggar stood at the mouth of the tunnel, slapping the back of every Welsh player leaving the field until Patchell approached him. He grabbed his deputy for a hug, pulled Patchell's head closer to his and gave some words of encouragement.

It was a moment that embodied everything that this group of players were about. Biggar was able to put personal disappointment to one side and encourage the man who had replaced him to do his best. After the break Patchell immediately nailed another drop-goal and you began to believe that this side really was different. They had learned their lessons from that decade-long run of defeats to Australia.

Then came the response from the Wallabies. Dane Haylett-Petty went over for a try that was converted by Matt Toomua – who had turned the game since replacing Bernard Foley – to get Cheika's side back within reach as the Wallabies took control of the second half. Wales were asked to hang on, and then some, as their opponents came roaring back into the contest, but we've seen it so many times before from Wales under Gatland and defence coach Shaun Edwards. Their sheer guts and determination makes them incredibly tough to break down. They can hang on for phase after phase in their own 22 when other teams would wilt. It's quite something to watch, and their defensive skills were really put to the test.

After 15 minutes of tackling, Michael Hooper found a crack in the wall of red jerseys and his converted try brought Australia back to within four points. I've sat in press boxes in the past and watched Wales lose games from this point – against Australia more often than not! – but everything we'd seen before suggested that this side were not a clone of their past. With 20 minutes to go, we would find out what they were really about.

Meanwhile, the small pockets of red all around the ground were doing their best to make their voices heard over the oceans of green and gold. It was a remarkable atmosphere and defensive stops were being celebrated like tries. We'd seen Wales ride the emotion of the crowd to see games out in Cardiff, and now the diminished number of Wales fans in Tokyo were doing their best to provide those waves of emotion on the other side of the world.

Toomua knocked over a penalty to bring his side to within a point and there seemed like there was only going to be one winner. This painful movie had been seen so many times before. It felt like the game was slipping away from Wales. The relentless Wallabies kept coming hard but Wales stayed composed and began to wrestle back control of the game. They showed incredible composure to work a penalty at the other end of the field. Patchell showed real bottle to knock it over, and Wales saw the game out.

The only other time Wales had beaten a southern hemisphere powerhouse at a World Cup was in 1987, which put this current crop of players in largely unexplored waters. They'd achieved something they'd never done under Gatland, which meant nobody really knew where this could take them but it must be somewhere good.

Despite my previous views that the game was not as pivotal as many made out, it became clear afterwards that the squad regarded it as a big win: "I said to the boys that I would like to see them celebrate tonight. They deserve to celebrate. It was a tough game and a great win," said Gatland afterwards. "The man next to me [Alun Wyn Jones] has become the record cap holder for Wales and we need to recognise that, but we've only won two games and we need to make sure we do a job in the other games. I want the guys to look after themselves tonight but they deserve to pat each other on the back and say well done. It was a tough game but a victory. It's confidence-boosting for the next couple of games."

The surge of self-belief within the squad, from being able to beat a foe that had turned them over so many times in the past, and on the biggest stage of all to boot, was palpable. There was a real feeling that this could be the springboard for something special, that there was no way they were not going to top Pool D and give themselves a preferable route to the final. They had a relatively clean bill of health and now they had a nine-day break before facing Fiji.

It would have been easy to start to get carried away at this point, but this was Wales. There was no way this tournament was going to play out with no more twists and turns. Either way, it was clear from that point that we were in for one hell of a ride.

8

Out of the Bubble

"I'm very lucky I didn't get on that plane."
Adam Beard

After the stunning win over the Wallabies, Wales now had complete control of Pool D and a nine day break to get their bodies right. They'd played two Test matches in six days and had to travel around 200 miles in between. They needed the rest but, fortunately, they were still in fairly good shape, which was key.

Liam Williams had rolled his ankle during the Australia game but was not a concern, whilst Adam Beard was still working furiously to get back to fitness after the surgery on his appendix. The main concern was Dan Biggar, who was going through the 'return to play' concussion protocols after being knocked out in Tokyo. Other than that, Wales had a relatively clean bill of health.

If you make it all the way to the end – and Wales had every intention of doing so – the Rugby World Cup is a long slog for players. The tournament lasts one day over six weeks – though most teams arrived over a week before the start – and, if you make it all the way, you play seven Test matches in that time. That itinerary places an incredible amount of stress on the players, not just physically but emotionally, which is often forgotten by supporters and those outside the game. We all see the strapping and the limping and the soreness, but the emotional toil isn't always apparent. It is absolutely crucial to the success of a team in tournaments like this that players peak and relax at the right times. It's impossible to maintain a constant state of emotional readiness for the entire trip, so it's vital players switch off from rugby when they get the chance.

With that in mind, after the Australia match, Wales packed their bags and travelled to Ōtsu. It was not a tournament city and, walking around the place, there was no sign of the Rugby World Cup. It was almost as if the tournament no longer existed. The idea was for the players to get themselves away from the competition for a few days and completely switch off – to get their bodies and minds right.

Warren Gatland has had success with this tactic on British and Irish Lions tours in the past. In 2013, he took the Lions to Noosa between the second and third Test matches to recharge their batteries and get away from the hustle and bustle of the tour. Then, four years later, he did the same thing, taking the tourists to Queenstown before the final Test match – with the series still in the balance – where the players relaxed and got away from rugby for the most part. These short breaks away from the bubble allow players to take stock, get perspective and put their bodies right for the final assault on the competition. It had clearly worked on those trips and the logic was sound.

Getting off the train in Ōtsu was the polar opposite to getting off the train in Shinjuku. It was as if we'd left Japan and were in a different country although we'd only travelled 280 miles.

There was very little happening. A few people milled around and a taxi or two sat at the curb but that was about it. Had tumbleweed rolled across the road in front of me, it would not have looked out of place.

So, what was there to do in Ōtsu? To be frank, not a lot. On the first day, one player went out with his family in search of good local cuisine and, after disappearing for an hour or so in a taxi, was told that the best place for food in the area was the Italian restaurant in the team hotel. The focal point of the area was the vast Lake Biwa, Japan's largest freshwater lake, stretching long beyond the horizon. It was breathtaking to look at and a lot of the hotels in the area, including Wales', were situated on its shores.

Whilst the lake was beautiful to look at, there wasn't a great deal to do on it, certainly not in the area where the players were staying. There were no sandy or grassy places where you could ease yourself into the gentle waves for a swim, but there was a fishing harbour and a concrete wall going around its banks.

To keep themselves busy, Hadleigh Parkes, Gareth Davies, Elliot Dee, Leigh Halfpenny, Rhys Carre and Liam Williams all had a little fishing trip sorted out by one of the team's liaison officers. Other players ventured up into the mountains, getting a breathtaking view of the lake and the city of Ōtsu, while some dabbled in the multi-storey games arcade and sports entertainment complex situated near the hotel. Outside of that, though, there wasn't much else on offer.

On the first full day in Ōtsu, Bradley Davies was put in front of the media. The second row, and flanker James Davies, are the two interviews that you always look forward to. Both are genuinely funny blokes and normally throw up something worth writing about.

A week or so earlier, I'd heard a tale about the 32-year-old leaving the squad's WhatsApp group in the wake of Wales' 22-17 defeat to Ireland in Cardiff. That game was Davies' one and only chance to impress the coaches but he struggled to impose himself on the match having not played in a Test match for over a year. He knew afterwards that he wasn't going to make the squad and, given his age and the emergence of Cory Hill and Adam Beard, perhaps pondered how many more chances he'd have to play for Wales. Not needing to be told, he removed himself from the group.

When Davies sat down in front of us, I put the question to him, thinking it would lead to a tales of banter, fines and a glorious return to the WhatsApp group, but I'd slightly misjudged it and my question caught Davies a little off-guard. When he answered, he obviously regretted it, which was not the response I was expecting: "Yeah. It was a mistake on my part," he said, "it's done now and I apologised. I was out in Cardiff with my friends and a bit of 'Dutch courage' came in. The boys have added me back in and I've had a bit of chat off them!"

That night, Wales were welcomed to the city by local political dignitaries – I got the impression Ōtsu didn't have international professional sports outfits visit often – out on the lake. It sounded like a great idea, initially, but around 45 minutes before the team were due to board the ship to go for a leisurely cruise, the weather turned vicious. Dark clouds rolled over the mountains that surrounded the city and suddenly the lightning cracked and the thunder boomed all around. I sent a text to the team's media manager to check if they were still going ahead with the trip. In upbeat fashion, he brushed off the weather and confirmed they were, but I thought to myself 'I'd rather you than me!'

The ship was packed with the dignitaries, their guests, local schoolchildren and the city's media. As they tended to at these engagements, the squad sang *Calon Lan* – a Welsh hymn – which always went down extremely well with their hosts, then they had a go at playing some traditional Japanese drums, which were 1,000 years old, and a good time was had by all. Outside, though, an almighty storm raged.

I'm fortunate enough to have visited Florida on a number of occasions and they get some particularly intense storms during the summer months, but that bout of thunder and lightning in Ōtsu eclipsed anything I'd ever witnessed in the USA. Totally oblivious to the storm, the trip continued without a hitch: "There were a few flashes in the windows but that was about it," smiled the media manager when I spoke to him the following day.

After arriving back on solid ground, the squad signed autographs and took pictures with the crowd that awaited them and, from my hotel room, I could hear the Welsh national anthem blaring out over the speakers. It was a yet another warm welcome in this friendly country.

The players arrived in Ōtsu on Tuesday, October 1 and were given a few days off before what they call 'Test week' began on Friday, October 4 – though there was an optional training session in the interim, which the majority of the squad attended. If a game is on a Saturday, Wales' 'Test week' under Gatland looked like this; Monday – training, Tuesday – training, Wednesday – day off, Thursday – team announcement and training, Friday – captain's run, Saturday – game, Sunday – day off. Most of those days would, though, involve weight training in the morning and work on the pitch in the afternoon or vice versa, and it will always be tinkered with slightly during a campaign depending on how the players are holding up.

Now if, like in a World Cup, the day of the game is moved, then the Test week moves. Wales played Fiji on Wednesday, October 9 so that week, the itinerary was; Friday – training (open to the public), Saturday – training, Sunday – travel day, Monday – team announcement and training, Tuesday – captain's run, Wednesday – game.

During the Friday (open) training session, Wales went through their usual drills and routines whilst the fans looked on and, after the session, there was a chance for the kids to get involved. Suddenly, hundreds of schoolchildren came streaming out of the changing room area wearing different colour bibs, then split up into barely manageable groups for the players to do some drills and play a game or two.

Owen Watkin, Josh Adams, Hadleigh Parkes, Justin Tipuric, George North, Leigh Halfpenny, Josh Navidi, Ryan Elias, Elliot Dee and Aaron Shingler all did their best to communicate their instructions, sometimes with the help of a translator or a liaison officer. This was no easy task for the players, who would probably have preferred a 20 stone Fijian running down their channel as an alternative, but they ploughed on through the significant language barrier and the children thoroughly enjoyed themselves.

To my left, Adams was plonking a ball down on a kicking tee with the children queuing up to whack the ball towards, and sometimes over, the posts. In front of me, North and Watkin had their group in two lines and racing to get the ball from one end to the other by passing it between their legs and over their shoulders. All over the field, various drills were taking place. It was another example of the squad engaging with the local community. Not all teams out in Japan did this sort of thing and it was clear how impressive this squad of players were off the field as well as on it. Not just in Ōtsu, but throughout the trip, they served as fantastic ambassadors for Wales as a nation and I'm not sure that was always recognised back home.

That week also saw one of the best interviews of the tour, and there were some great ones to compete with. The media sat down with Adam Beard in the cafe at the team hotel and everyone was keen to know just what sort of drama had unfolded on the day Wales flew to Tokyo, leaving Beard behind.

The second row had been feeling some pain in his stomach the day before Wales travelled, which he believed to be only a case of trapped wind. It turned out to be something far more serious. The pain got progressively worse on the bus journey up to Heathrow and the team doctor, Dr Geoff Davies, assessed Beard upon arrival at the airport and deemed him not fit to fly. Beard was put back on the team coach, with only the squad's bus driver for company, and taken straight to A&E at the Heath Hospital in Cardiff, where WRU physio John Miles was waiting to meet him. Within four hours, he was having surgery to remove his appendix.

Around half of the flight, maybe more, from London to Tokyo is spent going over Russia and, had Beard got on that plane, it is thought they would have almost certainly required an emergency landing. The gravity of the situation was not lost on the man himself: "It could have been dangerous," Beard told us. "I'm very lucky I didn't get on that plane. Geoff made the right call and the boys were bantering with him that finally he had made one right call. He was amazing all through the steps and I am lucky enough he made those calls."

Now that he was in Japan, Beard's mission was to pack on the weight he'd lost and get back up to speed. He was consuming around 5,000 calories a day and taking 'beastings' from strength and conditioning coach Huw Bennett. It spoke volumes of how highly the management group rated him that they even brought him back out to Japan. The Fiji game would come too soon for Beard, but coming it was.

From one second row to another, we were also given the chance to interview Jake Ball before we left Ōtsu. The Scarlet is arguably the most unglamorous and unheralded work horse in the squad but, in Japan, he was proving to be worth his weight in gold, and he's a big bloke.

74

What people often overlook with Ball is the fact that he has been through injury hell in the last few years and that's no exaggeration. With Cory Hill and Beard breaking onto the scene, Ball's absence has not been felt as heavily as it might have been, but he was back firing on all cylinders on the big stage at the World Cup and had overcome a remarkable amount of adversity to be there.

He suffered a shoulder dislocation against the All Blacks in 2017 and then, in the two years that followed, he got nerve damage as a result of the operation, ruptured his bicep, got concussed, injured his shoulder again and required foot surgery: "The most frustrating thing about my shoulder was that they said it was meant to be a four-month return," Ball told us.

"There was a point where it just wasn't getting any stronger. I had a hole in my back where the muscle had just stopped working because of the nerves that they disrupted. At one point, I wasn't sure that was going to get any better. As anyone knows with nerve injuries, they're just frustrating. With other rehab, you can rehab hard and get back quicker. With a nerve it comes back as quick as it wants to, there is nothing you can do to change that. I found that hard as I've never had an injury like that before." Every player has a story to tell, despite how unglamorous or unheralded they may be.

Before Wales travelled to their next destination, they had one final training session in Ōtsu, but were totally unprepared for what greeted them at the training ground. Once more, thousands of fans turned out to watch them. The stand at the Ojiyama Athletic Field was full and I got the impression that the response from the locals had far exceeded the hopes of the organisers.

Because Otsu wasn't a host city, hotels were very affordable. As a result of that, and by chance, I'd ended up staying in the same hotel as the team during those five nights. Once I'd realised the situation, I wasn't entirely sure how it was going to be received. Journalists staying in the same hotel as the team they're reporting on is nothing new, but my personal view is that there are certain boundaries you need to respect.

Many professional athletes are very wary of journalists and most have legitimate personal reasons for that. To the best of my knowledge, none of the players had issues with me personally but I still feared I was encroaching on their space. However, that week just strengthened my sense that this was a group of players who were comfortable in their own skin and were more than able to deal with the pressure they were under.

Players, and particularly backroom staff, made the effort to have a chat and were often quite interested to know what I'd experienced in Japan. Team manager Alan Phillips would often share recommendations for places to eat and that sort of information is invaluable when you're in a place that is difficult to navigate. It made covering the side a lot easier and was in stark contrast to the stories that were emerging from journalists covering other teams in the tournament, where reporters were treated with more than a degree of suspicion and, in some cases, disdain.

The Welsh players all knew that, if it was warranted, we would have to be critical at times and I've no doubt that their relaxed mood was facilitated by the fact we had no reason to throw shade on them because things could not have been going any better. I also got a greater understanding of the demands placed on players. Ōtsu felt pretty remote compared to many of the cities we visited throughout the trip, but even there autograph hunters and selfie-takers lay in wait. One local chap sat in the lobby every day the team were in town, getting players to sign their own picture in his book. He even approached me one day. Imagine his disappointment! I never found out how many autographs he managed to accrue over the course of

Wales' stay but I can guarantee that he was never turned away by a player.

Those few days gave me a real sense of just how calm and quietly confident Gatland's side were. Couple that with the fact that they'd just pulled off a real noteworthy victory over the Wallabies and, from where I was standing, things couldn't have been any better at that moment in time.

Everyone was in for a rude awakening.

9

Not Fiji, Not Again

"You've finally seen the light, have you?"
James Davies

After arriving in Ōita, we began hearing reports that a typhoon was heading towards Japan and was forecast to have a major impact on the tournament, particularly Pool A. Initial forecasts had it heading towards Fukuoka where Ireland were scheduled to play Samoa, putting the game in serious doubt.

In the event of a cancelled Pool match, the game is deemed a 0-0 draw and both teams get two tournament points. If Ireland's game were to be cancelled, it would have put Scotland's fate back in their own hands after a disappointing start to the competition. Scotland boss Gregor Townsend pointed out that the Ireland game should not be postponed or moved as per competition rules and, if it were to be cancelled, the points must be shared. Words he would later live to regret, if only for a brief moment.

Back in Wales camp, James and Jonathan Davies had been named to start against Fiji. It was the first time in 20 years that brothers had a represented Wales at a World Cup, with Scott and Craig Quinnell the last to do it in 1999. The younger of the two brothers, James, greeted news of his call-up in typical fashion, as Gatland revealed: "I said to James 'Well done' and he replied 'You've finally seen the light have you?' But then he said 'I'm only joking'. I loved that. I thought it was brilliant. It's a great response. I love a bit of banter like that and I have no problem with comments like that. It just says to me that players believe in their own ability. They want to be in the squad and they think they're good enough to be in the starting side. I thought that was a really good response."

Davies' selection, however, at the expense of Justin Tipuric, who was rested to captain the side against Uruguay just four days after the Fiji match, was considered a risk by many pundits. They assumed that Davies was selected because his sevens background would suit the style of play that Fiji would bring. That, though, wasn't the case. The management's thinking was that if Wales encountered injuries in the latter stages of the tournament, it would have been unfair to throw the larger-than-life Scarlet into the biggest game of his career having only faced Uruguay as preparation. Gatland simply wanted to give 'Cubby Boi' some game time against genuine opposition, with all due respect to *Los Teros*.

The Davies brothers were put up for interview together in front of the TV cameras. Having interviewed James in Argentina, I knew this had potential. Whilst we had to cover off questions about the game and the call-up, the best way to make this work was to get the brothers talking about each other.

Back in that rugby club just outside Buenos Aires, I remembered James joking that his parents hadn't made the trip because 'Goldenballs' (his brother) wasn't involved. I reminded him of that and then asked if his parents had made the trip to Japan: "Well they have but obviously he's here, so they've made the trip," he smiled. "I think they booked a while ago expecting Jon to be picked and they've ended up with two for the price of one now that I managed to make the squad. It's a big trip for them and I'm sure they'll be looking forward to the game."

Despite their desire to remain apart, the pair were forced to share a room when the squad first arrived in Tokyo a few weeks earlier: "It was a late change," explained James. "We had two beds pushed together to make a double so we had to separate them into single beds and I didn't have any sheets so I just had a plain duvet from the cupboard and a pillow." At that point Jonathan added: "I said the bath originally but I gave him half the bed."

Other than the Tipuric omission, it was pretty much as expected from Gatland, though Ross Moriarty was given the chance to start, with Aaron Wainwright on the bench for the first time. For most observers, this was set to be a stern test for Wales but one that they were eventually expected to pass with flying colours.

"They're a typical island side. When they get some confidence and belief, they're incredibly dangerous," said Gatland of Fiji. "They've got some real threats and we just have to make sure we focus on ourselves. We've had a good break and some good preparation leading into this game. We saw how dangerous they were against Australia in the first half. We've got to make sure we shut their space down, shut the time down on the ball and defend really well. Shaun has been speaking to the players about putting in an 80 minute performance defensively. We haven't done that yet. One of the pleasing things from the first two games is how well we've started. Our starts have been exceptional and it's important we start well on Wednesday and take a bit of that excitement away from Fiji."

To Gatland's credit, everything he said was on the money. Wales had to control the game, build a score early and withdraw any shred of hope, optimism or 'excitement' from their opponents early on. The longer Fiji felt they were in the game, the more interested they would be. It all sounded great but when Jérôme Garcès blew his whistle to start the match, chaos ensued.

Though the comparison is the easy one, it was depressingly reminiscent of Wales' embarrassing defeat to Fiji in 2007. The game was utterly frenetic, nobody had control of it, least of all Wales and that is exactly how Fiji boss John McKee had drawn it up. Within minutes, Josua Tuisova was given ample room and a one-on-one with Josh Adams. He bowled the Welshman over and squeezed the ball down in the corner despite the best efforts of Wales' cover defence.

Shortly after, Fiji were breaking down the left when Ken Owens put in a tip tackle on Viliame Mata and was sent to the sin bin. On another day, with a different referee, it could have been far worse.

Then Kini Murimurivalu was the next man to bundle over Adams on his way to the line. Fiji were 10-0 up after 11 minutes and had a one-man advantage. From my vantage point in the press box I, like many Wales fans, started thinking 'surely this isn't happening again'.

Then my mind turned to the week before, where Wales had been given a number of days off and completely switched off from the tournament. At the time it seemed like a great idea but had I misjudged that? Wales looked as though they were still on the shores of Lake Biwa, but the one thing that was always in the back of my mind was that this group of players had overcome worse starts. They'd already shown a resilience that had been absent in Wales squads of yesteryear. There was no doubting they had the potential to recover but could they actually pull it off?

I was loathed to make the comparison to 2007 because it felt a little lazy, but it was fitting. Wales were so loose and at times they got sucked into playing a game that suited Fiji. The

Fijian defence was aggressive and Wales started throwing speculative offloads on the back foot, compounding errors with more errors, exactly like they'd done 12 years previously. This was never in the script, Fiji had totally unsettled the team and blown apart Gatland's game plan.

To Wales' credit, they fought back into the game and they were helped as Fiji suffered a mini implosion. Tevita Cavubati was sin-binned for a dangerous clearout – again, on another day it could have been worse – and a minute later, Dan Biggar's inch-perfect cross kick found the arms of a soaring Adams, who dived over. Then, around the half hour mark, Semi Kunatani was sent to the sin bin and Wales struck again through Adams down the left. The conversion put Wales four points in front. Surely it would be smooth sailing from here, wouldn't it?

Despite the rip-roaring nature of the game, Wales lead 14-10 at the break, but Semi Radradra was roaming wherever he pleased and causing absolute havoc, a constant threat wherever he popped up. His presence was unsettling.

James Davies was sin-binned 10 minutes into the second half for killing the ball and, moments later, Fiji rumbled a maul towards the Welsh line. It collapsed and Garcès ran under the posts to award a penalty try. It's never easy.

Then came the moment for which the game will be remembered. After Fiji's penalty try, Dan Biggar was like a man possessed. He was fired up, chasing everything, determined to drag his side out of this mess, single-handedly if he had to. He was making tackles, bouncing straight back up, and looking for his next job with particular enthusiasm. Murimurivalu chipped the ball in behind and suddenly time began to slow down. As soon as I realised what was about to unfold. I just looked at my keyboard, I didn't need to see what was about to happen, even if I did force myself to watch the replays. At the end of the day I had to report on it.

Biggar was retreating, eyes only for the ball, and Liam Williams was storming forward with his eyes on the same object. Williams rose slightly off the ground to claim it and Biggar did not. The full-back's shoulder hit Biggar on the side of the head, spinning him violently off balance, towards the ground. As he fell, William's hip caught Biggar in the head on the way down. The collision left the fly-half lying motionless on the pitch.

Play was stopped and Williams was on one knee, roughly 10 metres away from Biggar, staring at his team-mate, who was being tended to by medics. After a few minutes of treatment, Biggar rose to his feet and jogged off the pitch and down the tunnel, leading a trail of physios, first aiders, and staff carrying a spinal board. He never returned.

Once again, Rhys Patchell was thrown into the cauldron but, unlike his appearance against Australia, Wales were behind and he had to turn the game around. Just like in Tokyo, though, his first meaningful contribution was to knock over a penalty and it brought Wales level. Enter Jonathan Davies.

The two-time British and Irish Lion had been playing well all tournament but he now produced his trademark hand-off to break away from the defence and then raced into the Fiji 22. Radradra came across to tackle him but Davies got away a lovely offload to Adams, who went over in the corner.

I never felt that finish from Adams got enough credit. He was off balance and had to launch himself over Davies and Radradra, essentially nose-diving into the turf. The winger had been culpable for Wales conceding two tries earlier in the match but he had now claimed a hat-trick of his own. Adams and Davies both required attention after the try, and although Adams, who we later learned had suffered a dead leg, carried on with his quad muscle heavily strapped, it was a different story for Davies. He retreated to the sideline, sat on the bench and put his head in his hands. Not a sight Wales fans wanted to see. The tackle look innocuous and, at this point, I didn't have the impression his injury was too serious, though he would certainly now miss the Uruguay game.

Back on the field, Williams scored a bonus point try to wrap things up and gave his trademark 'relax' celebration to the crowd, though I'd suggest anyone watching in red was doing anything but that. Fiji were still in the mood for an upset, with Radradra probing dangerously at every occasion, but Wales saw the game out and booked their place in the quarter-finals with a 29-17 win. They'd made it three from three but at what cost?

Biggar had been given a head injury assessment and removed from play meaning he would have to go through the protocols, thus ruling him out of the Uruguay game, while Davies would be sent for scans. It would be a nervy couple of days for him, and Wales had just 96 hours to patch themselves up after an immensely physical encounter with the Fijians. They'd made hard work of their victory and their bodies were battered.

In hindsight, the Fiji game was the start of Wales' problems. A number of bodies had been knocked around, and even those who finished the game were suffering after a very physical battle. Fiji may have lost the game but they certainly left their mark on a Wales team who'd made life difficult for themselves.

As they travelled to Kumamoto, Typhoon Hagibis, which had now veered north, directly hit Tokyo. As a result, two games, that were scheduled to be played on Saturday, October 12 were cancelled; England v France (Yokohama) and New Zealand v Italy (Toyota City). It was the first time in the tournament's 32-year history that organisers had been forced to cancel matches. Ireland's game against Samoa in Fukuoka, on Japan's south island, was unaffected and went ahead as planned.

Suddenly, though, given that the typhoon had changed its course, Scotland's game against Japan in Yokahama was now under serious threat of being cancelled, a matter of days after Townsend's comments. If it were to be called off, it would leave Ireland needing just a draw against Samoa to book their place in the knockout stages at Scotland's expense. A war of words ensued with a furious Scottish Rugby Union threatening legal action, and SRU chief executive Mark Dodson telling the BBC Radio 4's *Today* that he would not let "Scotland be the collateral damage for a decision that was taken in haste".

This was all unfolding hundreds of miles away as I travelled between Ōita and Kumamoto, but the gravity of what was heading towards Japan had dawned on me. Typhoon Hagibis was predicted to be the worst that had hit the country in decades, it posed a genuine threat to the lives of those who fell in its path and tournament organisers were dealing with an almost unprecedented situation.

Though I found it easier to gather perspective, given I was covering Wales and not Scotland, the Scots' game against Japan went ahead and they were thumped out of the tournament, losing 28-21 to the hosts. Namibia v Canada, which was due to take place in Kamaishi – 550 miles away from Toyota City, where the All Blacks were supposed to face Italy – was also cancelled.

At the time this book was completed, 88 people were confirmed to have lost their lives in the typhoon and CNN has estimated that Hagibis caused $9 billion (USD) worth of damage. Hagibis never impacted on Wales, who were over 700 miles south of Tokyo preparing to face Uruguay in Kumamoto but, as the tournament continued, those few days gave us all a bit of perspective.

Given the way the cancelled games had impacted on the tournament, however, barring the unthinkable against Uruguay, Wales would avoid meeting England in the quarter-finals. This was probably the first time I gave serious thought to the fact that, in a few short weeks, we could potentially have a Wales v England Rugby World Cup final, but there was a lot of rugby to be played before that.

The short break between matches left little time for media access in Kumamoto, and the tournament was really rattling on at some speed. In fact, the first time we saw anyone from the Wales camp was the day that Gatland announced his team.

The four-day turnaround saw the Wales head coach make 13 changes to the starting side that had beaten Fiji, with Hadleigh Parkes and Josh Adams the only two asked to 'go again'. Before the games, Shaun Edwards was put before the media and asked why Wales were suddenly missing an uncharacteristic amount of tackles.

For years, Wales' success had been built on their defence but Fiji had cut them open with ease. I was expecting a tense exchange when another journalist put the point to Wales' fiery defence coach, but it didn't happen: "When you're playing teams who are in the top 12 ranked teams, it would be very unusual not to concede a try," said Edwards. "When you're playing teams ranked a lot lower than that, maybe it's a game in which you are capable of keeping the opposition try-less, but all I know is that a lot of the rules – and I'm not saying it's a bad thing, it's probably good for the game – are pro-attack. I think if you look throughout world rugby over the last couple of years, the amount of points being scored... in Super Rugby you see scores like 38-47. There will be more points scored, there's no doubt about that."

Official stats had Wales missing 32 tackles against Fiji and, whilst Edwards' figures differed, he was quick to praise Fiji: "I looked at that stat myself and realised we missed 25 tackles, then I thought to myself, who did we miss those tackles on?" said Edwards. "Then I looked and there were 16 missed tackles on both of their wingers who, let's be honest, are not the easiest human beings to tackle. If anyone has an A to Z on how to tackle Josh Tuisova, please send me it. They are incredible athletes, [but] obviously there were too many [missed tackles]. We only missed nine tackles on the rest of the team. Those two wingers are exceptional."

Against Uruguay, though, defence was the glaring issue in what was a disjointed Welsh performance. Making 13 changes to a side will always have an adverse effect on it – you lose all the continuity and the familiarity that has been built up over time. *Los Teros* were perhaps more stubborn than they had been given credit for and made things difficult, but Wales also contributed to making the game difficult for themselves. They couldn't find any rhythm and there were countless handling errors and mistakes.

Nicky Smith had burrowed over for a try, converted by Leigh Halfpenny, but Wales couldn't settle and only carried a 7-6 lead into half time. Normally, the plucky minnows are a crowd pleaser but there was something about the way Uruguay conducted themselves that day that made them hard to like.

As the clock went dead at the end of the first half, Hadleigh Parkes kicked the ball into touch to head into the sheds and take stock, rather than continue to batter away at the Uruguayans. It prompted *Les Teros* captain Juan Manuel Gaminara to jump up and down before shouting in Aled Davies' face.

Gaminara then chased Parkes off the field and was about to give him a mouthful too before Ross Moriarty intervened and nudged the Uruguayan, ushering him away from Parkes. The Uruguay skipper then slipped on the plastic covering at the mouth of the tunnel and some pushing and shoving followed towards the dressing room.

After the break Josh Adams went over for his fifth try of the group stages but still Uruguay refused to surrender. Wales couldn't bury the game and that wasn't helped by a hat-trick of disallowed Hallam Amos tries. A penalty try on the hour mark stretched their lead but Uruguay hooker German Kessler went over for a score of his own that will have, no doubt, frustrated Shaun Edwards. Tomos Williams sniped to score with six minutes remaining and then Gareth Davies, who came off the bench as a winger, scored a lovely solo effort to round off the 35-13 win in style. Bradley Davies, who had joined the tour as a late injury call-up for Cory Hill, finished the game as captain of the side, taking over when Tipuric was replaced in the 58th minute.

What was missed by everyone in the stadium at the time though, was that in the aftermath of Williams' try, Uruguay replacement Guillermo Pujadas had spat at the Wales scrum-half. The Welsh management referred the incident, which was one of a few that had occurred 'off the ball', to the citing commissioner and Pujadas was later banned for six weeks. The notes from Pujadas' hearing made for pretty remarkable reading as he accepted the offence warranted a red card but insisted he could not remember the incident.

Unfortunately for him, Rhys Patchell saw the whole thing and remembered it vividly: "As Gareth Davies ran in his try I saw Tomos Williams and the Uruguay six having a bit of a scuffle. Nothing to it particularly," said Patchell. "Then 16 blue got involved as there was pushing and shoving from both sides. As everybody parted, I saw 16 blue spit at Tomos Williams. I can't tell whether it connected but I felt the intent was clear. I went straight to the ref to report this, but as it was the end of the game I'm not [sure] he clocked what it was I was saying. He seemed very intent on calming everyone down – understandable given the situation."

In 2016, Pujadas had been banned for five weeks for dissent towards an official. As they handed down his six-week punishment three years later, the judiciary panel concluded that "the player has a significant issue with the core rugby value of respect".

As for Wales, there were few players who had put their hand up against Uruguay to start the quarter-final against France. Before every game, Shaun Edwards sets the team a defensive target, which varies depending on the strength of the opposition. As we came to understand it, he wanted to keep Uruguay tryless but the minnows had scored. He was furious and let the players know about it in the dressing room after the match in no uncertain terms.

The performance had not been inspiring and it reminded me a lot of the Italy game during the 2019 Six Nations. Wales made 10 changes for that match and they stuttered to victory. You have to temper your criticism of these performances, though. Fans want to see Wales stick 70 points on teams like Uruguay and, if Gatland had decided to play a full strength side, I've no doubt that would have happened, but when you make so many changes and select unfamiliar combinations, things won't always work like they're supposed to. The individual errors were disappointing but the team that faced Uruguay was sent out there to win whilst protecting the frontline players. They performed that role, even if it wasn't the prettiest display.

However, Wales remained the only side in the tournament – having fulfilled every fixture – to win all their matches, and topped Pool D. It was the first time since 1987 that Wales had won all their Rugby World Cup Pool matches, but what sort of shape were they in?

After the match we learned that the scan of Jonathan Davies' left knee had come back clear, which was positive even if he wasn't yet fully recovered. Meanwhile, Dan Biggar's scan, after suffering concussions in two consecutive matches, also came back clear but he also had further work to do in order to prove his fitness.

Since the beginning of the Gatland era, and perhaps for the first time ever, Wales had never progressed to this stage of the tournament and looked in such good shape. Performances had waned slightly in the last two outings but they appeared to be on their way back to full health and had won four from four. If you'd have offered Gatland that at the start of the tournament, he'd have bitten your hand off.

"We are in a good place and building some momentum nicely," said Gatland after the match. "It was good for those players to get a run out today and, talking to the medics, they are hopeful that in a couple of days we will be able to get everyone fit and available for selection – the whole 31 training. That will be the first time we've had that out here which is really good and now it's about creating momentum.

"We've got a good record against France but they're traditionally a tournament team. In World Cups, when everyone writes them off, they seem to produce performances nobody expects. We know how hard next week is going to be against France. We have seen them play better against the better sides and France are going to be tough, but obviously we have a good record against them in recent years and a lot of success, but we cannot take that for granted. They probably have a little advantage, not having that game against England, so they may be a little bit fresher than we will be, but from our point of view we feel battle-hardened having come through four games."

10

Gallic Madness

"We have to count ourselves a bit lucky but if you want my honest opinion, I couldn't care less."
Dan Biggar

The win over Uruguay was not one that would live long in the memory. Of all the fringe players who were given the opportunity to impress, most failed to take that chance, though there were one or two noticeable performances.

Leigh Halfpenny showed flashes of some of his best form, counter-attacking from full-back and marshalling the backfield with typical game awareness. Few players read the game better. Another noteworthy performance was that of 21-year-old Rhys Carre who, in the 29 minutes he had off the bench, did more than anyone to make Warren Gatland take note.

His ball-carrying ability really was impossible to ignore, even if he was still slightly raw at the set piece. Carre's work in open play was a real point of difference – which Gatland craves in his players – when compared to the other loose-heads in the side, but Halfpenny and Carre were the only two who really made a case to start in the quarter-final.

One player who headed into the knockout stages in fine form was winger Josh Adams. He'd scored five tries in the four group games, making him the tournament's joint top try-scorer with Japan's Kotaro Matsushima after the Pool stage. Adams' try tally now left him just one short of legend Shane Williams' record for the most tries scored by a Welshman at a World Cup, the 87-cap hot-stepper having crossed for six tries during the 2007 tournament.

With potentially three games remaining, Adams also had a very real chance of chasing down the record for most tries in a single tournament, currently jointly held by All Blacks icon Jonah Lomu, Julian Savea and South Africa's Bryan Habana, who have all bagged eight tries in one tournament: "It wouldn't be bad to join that list, would it?" Adams pondered after the Uruguay game. "There are some legends there. It's always nice to get a try. It would be nice if I could join that list, but most importantly we need to win the games first."

For Adams to be thriving on this stage was such a great story as, just three years prior, he was trying to prove his worth to Worcester Warriors, having been sent out on loan to Cinderford in England's National League One South. This move to England came after he was deemed surplus to requirements at the Scarlets academy and no other Welsh region showed an interest. Now, here he was chasing down a record held by some of the game's greatest players. With his razor-sharp finishing, Adams was lighting up the tournament and it was the stuff of fairytales.

The gritty reality of tournament rugby was to the fore, however, as we arrived back in Ōita for the quarter-final showdown with *Les Bleus*, when it became apparent that Wales were a little more banged up than many back home might have realised, particularly the two players who had to start against Fiji and then Uruguay four days later.

Quite how close to being 100% fully fit Adams was remained to be seen after he suffered that dead leg against Fiji and played with it heavily-strapped against Uruguay. As for Hadleigh Parkes, he suffered a shoulder injury in the game in Kumamoto and it was more debilitating than it first appeared. This was on top of the broken bone he'd suffered in his hand against Georgia, but the stories of the week on the injury front were sure to be about Dan Biggar's recovery from the concussion he suffered against Fiji and Jonathan Davies' knee. George North, meanwhile, was battling an ankle injury but I never got the impression that was going to stop him playing in a World Cup quarter-final.

The day we arrived in Ōita, French newspaper *Midi Olympique* published a piece raising question marks over Biggar's potential participation in the quarter-final on the grounds that he had suffered two concussions in two matches. I thought the article was a little unfair. Personally, I have no doubt that nobody on the WRU's medical staff would sanction putting a player back on the field before he was ready to do so. WRU medical manager Prav Mathema has been vocal on the sport's battle with concussions over the years and championed the Union's 'recognise and remove' mantra at all levels of the game in Wales.

As we learned later that week, Biggar was put through stringent testing before being cleared for action.

On the Tuesday before the France clash, Wales issued a fitness update via attack coach Stephen Jones, who revealed Biggar and North had both returned to training. Jonathan Davies, meanwhile, was being phased back into preparations for the quarter-final: "We're in a great position. The boys integrated back into training today," said Jones. "The medical team have done a fantastic job on our players. From a squad selection point of view, it's brilliant. Dan is good to go. He is training with us today, which is fantastic. I am not too sure about Jon's medical condition, but from a coach's perspective, I am just glad he is back training and healthy. You want a full complement. You look at those players, huge experience, great skillset, Jon has a physical threat and you saw what he did with that last linebreak just before he got injured. Wonderful offload as well. It's vital we have everyone fit and healthy."

It sounded positive but I had my suspicions, as did many of the travelling journalists. We were never able to quite get to the bottom of exactly what Davies had done to his knee, and the way in which he'd suffered the injury was so nondescript that we would have been simply guessing the diagnosis, given our viewpoint from high in the stand. Whenever the question was raised at press conferences the interviewee never gave much away, which only fuelled the speculation and, such was Davies' importance to the side, the rugby journalists started to compare the situation to when David Beckham fractured his metatarsal before the 2002 FIFA World Cup.

Given the significance of the player and the occasion, I made the effort – every chance I got – to traipse up into the hills above Beppu to watch some of Wales' training sessions, in the fear that the one day I didn't bother, something might happen. Media are given access to around 15 minutes of training on most days during the build-up to a World Cup match but it is very much an exercise for broadcasters to get their cutaway shots and little else. I always went up with my video camera as a significant part of my role for *WalesOnline* in Japan was to send back as much video material as I could, and we discovered that our readers really enjoyed watching clips of the training sessions.

The truth, though, was that as rugby journalists we never really got to see a lot in those 15-minute media sessions. Players will go through individual warm preparations, then there will be a squad warm-up and some stretching before going into some passing. It's at this point that journalists and their cameras are ushered away.

I was getting texts and calls all week about Jonathan Davies, not just from the office in Cardiff, but from my mates back home as well. Everybody wanted to know exactly what the latest was, how he looked in training, whether he was going to be fit for Sunday. I was well-placed to give an opinion on that but I always had a nagging doubt in the back of my mind. As soon as we were ushered away, Davies could well have just sat in the large tent erected near the training pitch, taken his strapping off and watched the others train. I had no idea whether he ever did that but I knew it was a distinct possibility. All week I made sure to play it safe with my reports in the event that we could all have been led down a garden path.

Throughout the week, with that left leg heavily strapped, Davies continued to train in front of the cameras and appeared to be moving pretty well. A WRU source that week was adamant that all was well: "I guarantee you that 10, 12, 13 and 14 will all be fit." Those numbers obviously referring to Biggar, Parkes, Davies and North. I remained cautious.

Another theme for the week, as far as the French media were concerned, was Shaun Edwards. The defence guru had been heavily-linked with a move to the French national side after his job was done with Wales following the World Cup, although nothing had been confirmed. One French journalist had a question to Liam Williams shut down early in the week because of the way it was framed, and although questions about Edwards were not off limits, questions about what 'he will bring to France' were, because nothing had been officially announced.

The full-back is one of the top interviewees in the squad. He is up there as one of the most personable in a generally relatable squad of players, and had enjoyed a remarkable season, winning the Grand Slam, English Premiership and European Champions Cup. Many people also now know that he used to struggle with a stammer that prevented him from effectively putting his point across to journalists.

I interviewed him during the summer camp to Switzerland and was impressed by how much he'd improved in that aspect. Here he now was in Wales' team hotel, surrounded by a gaggle of about 15 journalists, relaxed as can be and cracking jokes. He spoke of the work he has done to get his emotions in check and how his move to join Saracens in London has seen him grow not only as a player but as a person.

In the past, Williams had been prone to letting his blood run too hot. His shoulder charge on Cornal Hendricks in 2014 resulted in a penalty try, costing Wales a first ever win over the Springboks in South Africa, and as recent as 2018, he was yellow carded for a high tackle on Matteo Minozzi. It was a character flaw that Gatland had been keen to eradicate for years.

There is nothing malicious about Williams, but since he has learned to curb that enthusiasm he has flourished into one of the best players in the world: "With age, I guess, and a bit of experience of playing outside Wales and with different people," said Williams when he was asked how he's learned to control those emotions. "I was with Scarlets for six years and leaving Wales to go and play in London was great. I've learned a lot about myself – and that's not just on the pitch, it's off as well. Hopefully it shows on the pitch. Maybe I've matured a bit."

There had been an increasing amount of talk about the fact that some teams were heading into the knockout stages with a two-week break after their final Pool matches were cancelled, while others had played four matches in a relatively tight timetable. This was not a topic that Williams was particularly interested in as he gave a typically matter-of-fact response to a question on the topic: "It doesn't really bother me, to be honest," he said. "If we have to play, we have to play. I'm not really fussed. I'll go upstairs now, have a game of cards or play on my PlayStation." Fair enough.

Two days before the game, Wales' team was named and it was at full strength. Just as the WRU source had hinted, Biggar, Parkes, Davies and North were all fit to start ... for now. In the press release sent out to journalists that reveals the selected team, the WRU added a section to the bottom, outlining exactly what Biggar had been required to do in order to be passed as fit to play in the match:

> 'Following Dan Biggar's concussion sustained in an accidental collision in the match against Fiji, the WRU have worked collaboratively with World Rugby to deliver the highest level of care for Dan.
>
> Dan has remained symptom free since the game and has completed the graduated return to play with no issues. Management has included MRI scanning and two consultations with a globally renowned Independent Concussion Consultant from Australia.
>
> We are pleased to say that given that all return to play protocols have been met, imaging being normal and ratification from the Independent Concussion Consultant, that Dan has been deemed fit to play.
>
> The WRU continues to ensure that player welfare is at the fore of our decision making processes and is independent of the any team or competition.'

Gatland was pressed on the matter in his press conference that followed, an hour after the team was announced, but largely reiterated what was in the press release, though he did add that Biggar had been fit for four days prior to the announcement and insisted that they'd "covered all the bases".

Later in the press conference, the Wales boss was quizzed on the 'do or die' nature of the tie against *Les Bleus*. This was innocently asked by the reporter, who was using a phrase that is often used in association with knockout matches. However, earlier that week, England boss Eddie Jones came in for some criticism when he used the phrase publicly. The negative response came in light of what had happened during Typhoon Hagibis and Gatland was not prepared to go down that same road.

It seemed Gatland had discovered the little bit of perspective that I thought had got lost in the week when the games were cancelled. "I wouldn't be using words like do or die. I think it's a bit sensitive at the moment, given what's happened in the last few weeks," explained Gatland. "It's just another game of rugby but we know how important it is. We're very focused on wanting to go out there and stay in this tournament. There is a lot of confidence in this squad. We feel we haven't given an 80-minute performance yet. We've been good in patches. We've been building nicely this week. We've had three really good sessions."

Such are the media demands placed on teams at the World Cup, players are made available for interview six out of the seven days a week but you will see some players more than others. Hadleigh Parkes is a press officer's dream. He's a great talker and, though he only has two years of experience on the international scene, the 32-year-old has enough years behind him to keep himself out of hot water. A well-travelled guy, Parkes is as interesting as they come but if you see the same person multiple times in a matter of weeks, it can be difficult to know what to ask next.

I, along with a number of other journalists, decided the best way to conduct the interview before the France game was to delve into his journey from Hunterville, New Zealand, to representing Wales in a Rugby World Cup quarter-final. To build the story, I wanted to get some real detail on how incoming Wales boss Wayne Pivac coaxed him over from New Zealand to play for the Scarlets before going into qualifying for Wales on residency and his path to international recognition.

"There were two options on the table – Bayonne for six months as a medical joker and maybe a little bit longer, or a two and a half year gig in west Wales," explained Parkes. "Wayne Pivac was my Auckland ITM Cup coach and then he got the job at Scarlets. He had been in touch a couple of times before he left and then it came through that there was a gig there and would I be keen? It was a great opportunity for both Suzy [now Parkes' wife] and myself to go. Suzy had just qualified as a chartered accountant so it was a bit tough to ask her to go to a French-speaking country where she probably wouldn't be able to work. For both of us it was probably a better move to go somewhere where she could work as well and get experience. She has loved that side of it."

Had the centre opted to head to Bayonne all those years ago rather than Parc Y Scarlets, he may well have been lining up in blue at Ōita Stadium that weekend. It's strange how things work out.

The following day, on the 'captain's run', trouble was on the horizon. The players had come out and started going through their usual individual stretches and then the team warm-up with some passing interspersed. As he had done all week, Jonathan Davies took part in all this right on the other side of the field, as far away from the cameras and journalists as possible, meaning we all struggled to get a decent view of him in action. He's not dull.

Just as the press were getting ready to leave, myself and another journalist spotted Davies stop what he was doing and consult with medic Prav Mathema before walking away from the session and heading into the tent at the side of the pitch. On his way, he walked past Gatland and muttered a few words to him. When we checked it out, we were told he had been taken away to do individual training in order to get more volume in his legs before the match, given he'd had a pretty light training week. This sowed further seeds of doubt in my mind. I saw some logic in what I was being told but I didn't buy it for one second, though I had no concrete evidence to suggest anything different.

Meanwhile at the final press conference before the match, Josh Adams, another of the squad's top interviewees, was addressing suggestions from France winger Yoann Huget that Wales played boring rugby. Adams was not concerned by Huget's comments given that Wales had scored 17 tries in their four Pool matches while France had only managed nine in their three matches: "Everyone's got an opinion," said Adams. "Maybe in the past we've kept games a little bit closer and kicked a little bit more ball, but that's dependent on the game plan and how we look at the opposition. You identify areas where you can put teams under pressure, and if that's keeping things tight with the forwards and putting more boot to ball, that's what we'll do. I definitely think in the last four games we've moved the ball quite well and have scored some good tries, actually. It's another string to our bow. We not only can grind teams down with the pack we've got, dominate aerially with the kicking game, but we can also move the ball around and use our threats in the backs. It's nice to keep teams guessing sometimes, whether we're going to come hard with the pack or shift it wide."

Immediately after that press conference I headed out to Ōita Stadium for the first quarter-final of the weekend between England and Australia. Having only recently comprehended that a Wales v England final was a distinct possibility, I wanted to get a closer look at Eddie Jones' side. It was an awesome performance from England, who took the Wallabies to the cleaners in every facet of the game, winning 40-16. It sent a real message to the other teams in the competition and Wales would have to respond the following day.

The atmosphere on matchdays in the knockout stages were always a little peculiar as there were plenty of neutral fans in and around the grounds. A lot of supporters hedged their bets on their team making it to certain stages of the tournament and had been let down by their side. It meant that there were always a few inside the ground who cared little which way the game went, they were just there for the experience. As such, the games didn't have as tribal a feel about them but Wales remained well-supported into the latter rounds of the tournament.

This was evidenced when I ventured to the fanzone in Ōita on the day of the quarter-final. There was red everywhere, again, and they mingled with the locals, with the French and with fans of every other nation. Rugby fans are able to come together like no other and it's always brilliant to see them mixing and sharing a beer. It was a great atmosphere but newfound friends were about to become enemies.

When I arrived at my seat in the press box about 90 minutes before kick-off, another UK-based journalist asked me if I was confident of Wales' chances. I was, and I had been for most of the games that had come before it for the previous two years. This squad of players had given me little reason to doubt them so I was upbeat about their chances. They were also playing against France, a familiar opposition who they'd beaten seven out of the last eight times they'd tried. Within minutes of our conversation ending, the news broke.

Jonathan Davies was out of the match after aggravating his knee injury during the 'captain's run'. Owen Watkin was starting.

My mind was instantly cast back to 24 hours previously as I watched Davies consult with Mathema before walking away from training. Had I seen him pulling out of the match there and then? To this day, I still don't know for certain but it was one hell of a coincidence if I hadn't. My confidence levels had dropped somewhat following the news. Watkin is a good player but he is not Jonathan Davies and this was by far the biggest occasion of his career, and he would be standing opposite Vrimi Vakatawa, no easy task.

If my confidence in Wales' ability to win the game had taken a hit before the match, imagine what I was thinking after 10 minutes. Early tries from Sébastien Vahaamahina and Charles Ollivon had France 12-0 ahead and cruising. Wales were caught in the headlights and it was all unravelling. Everyone knew *Les Bleus* had a big performance in them having not really shown much in the tournament to date and, typically, they seemed to find it when it really mattered.

A scrambling intervention from George North, who raced back towards his own line and miraculously gathered the loose ball and avoided being shoved back over his own whitewash, limited the damage. Jake Ball put in a thunderous shot on Guilhem Guirardo after 12 minutes, dislodging the ball for Aaron Wainwright to scoop it up and sprint away from the out-of-position French back three to score near the sticks. Biggar converted and then added a penalty as Wales began to slowly creep their way back into things.

Then came a heartbreaking moment for Josh Navidi. Approaching the half-hour mark, he made his way to the sideline to be replaced by Ross Moriarty. I hadn't seen any incident but whenever someone comes off that early in a match, it's usually the worst kind of news. We later learned that he'd suffered a hamstring injury that would end his tournament prematurely.

A fired-up Moriarty entered the fray having been kept on the bench for a lot of the action in Japan. He'd not been on the field for a minute before he was in trouble. He raced to the far side of the field to close down Gaël Fickou but got it wrong and ended up catching the centre on the chin as he attempted to make the tackle. Referee Jaco Peyper consulted his TMO Marius Jonker. Moriarty breathed a sigh of relief as Peyper dug out his yellow card and not his red one, but it had totally wrecked the momentum Wales had worked so hard to build after their horror start.

With the back-rower in the sin bin, France didn't take long to make their numerical advantage pay with Vakatawa diving over two minutes after Moriarty had been sent to the naughty chair. Some more vital interventions from Josh Adams kept France to just the one try while the Dragons back-rower was in the bin.

Just before the break, Romain Ntamack hit the upright with a penalty to give Wales a sniff but little was going in their favour. Wales were only nine points behind but it felt as though the deficit was twice as much as that. I was there in Paris when Wales miraculously recovered from 16-0 down to win. I'd also watched them turn things around against Fiji a little over a week previously, but I thought to myself that you can only pull so many rabbits out of the hat until the hat is empty. They'd had their chance to get back into the game and Moriarty's yellow card had seen to that.

Having been working relentlessly and following the team's every move, it dawned on me that I could be on a flight back to Heathrow within 48 hours. At least I'd get to see my girlfriend and family a bit sooner than I'd anticipated! I'd starting to plot out my piece for *WalesOnline*. The intro was going to read: 'It wasn't supposed to end this way.' Wales going out in the quarter-finals would be a disaster. Anything less than a semi-final would have been totally unsatisfactory. Gatland later admitted he was having similar thoughts during the match.

I appreciate this all seems a little downbeat but Wales were comfortably second best. Whatever the game plan was, they hadn't been able to impose it on the French, who were rampant. *Les Bleus* seemed to carry all the momentum in attack and defence, stifling anything Wales tried to get going. Wales had scored an opportunistic try but offered little else.

Nine minutes into the second half, though, the game was spun on its head. Most people in the ground missed it live but as soon as a replay of Vahaamahina elbowing a helpless Aaron Wainwright square in the jaw, apparently unprovoked, in the middle of the maul, we all knew what was coming next. Peyper had no choice but to show the French lock a red card. To call it a moment of madness would be doing it a disservice. It was stupidity beyond the realms of human comprehension.

Wales were virtually on the plane home with their tail between their legs and Vahaamahina had given them a lifeline. Four minutes later, Biggar kicked a penalty to get Wales back to within six points, but a frustrating, pointless, 20 minutes followed. Try as they might, Wales could not crack the French and, if anything, *Les Bleus* still looked a great threat despite being a man down.

It was reminiscent of when Wales failed to score against Australia in the 2015 World Cup when the Wallabies were down to 13 men. They simply couldn't stretch France at all and reverted to a very simple game plan. They made the conscious decision to take France on in the tight, where they were a man light, and became very direct, carrying hard off nine and 10 instead of going to the wide channels. At first glance it appeared that they'd gone into their shells under the pressure of needing another try, but this was by design: purposefully keeping it tight and trying to bludgeon their way through. It began to look as though that was a tactical decision they would live to regret for the rest of their careers.

In the final 10 minutes, Vakatawa barged through Dan Biggar and stormed into the Wales 22 but somehow they managed to hold on. With time winding down, they won a penalty and the fly-half booted the ball deep into French territory. The men in red attacked close to the French line but spilled it forward. French scrum.

That appeared to be it, the chance has gone but young props Rhys Carre and Dillon Lewis, either side of Ken Owens, produced a huge scrum to put France in some trouble. *Les Bleus* bolstered their depleted scrum with Gaël Fickou but the Wales forwards quickly gained momentum and, as Charles Ollivon – the French flanker playing number eight – gathered the ball he was enveloped by replacement scrum-half Tomos Williams who ripped the ball free, sending it flying up into the air.

Justin Tipuric pounced and drove to within inches of the line. Ross Moriarty – the villain less than an hour ago – was now the hero as he picked the ball up from the back of the ruck and dived over. Referee Peyper consulted with TMO Jonker and decided the rip had not gone forward before awarding the try to Wales. Biggar nervelessly slotted the conversion and, in the 74th minute, Wales took the lead for the first time.

Elliot Dee was thrown into the cauldron with just five minutes remaining as Wales went on to win a penalty at a crucial scrum. They kicked to the corner, Dee found Adam Beard at the lineout and the clock ticked into the red zone as Biggar booted the ball high into the stand to signal the end of the game. Cue wild celebrations.

How on earth had Wales managed to do that? They had no right to win the game but, somehow, they had. They were simply undeniable. They were staying out in Japan until the end of the tournament now, come what may. Afterwards, it wasn't lost on me that we'd seen the 'No Regrets' plan come to fruition in Ōita that night. There were nine Wales players on the field at the final whistle who had made their international debuts in the previous two years, namely: Carre, Dee, Lewis, Beard, Wainwright, T Williams, Parkes, Watkin and Adams. Watkin had huge boots to fill but had acquitted himself admirably. Without setting the game alight, he made few mistakes and fulfilled his role.

Wainwright was also worthy of a mention. He'd been playing outstanding rugby all tournament but Gatland kept pulling him off early in the second half of games. We could never get a coach to tell us exactly why this was but I speculated that, because of his age, they didn't feel he could maintain a level of performance for 80 minutes at this level just yet. But the injury to Navidi meant he had to go the distance in Ōita and he dug in with the rest of the team.

Quite frankly, how anyone performed was irrelevant as this was knockout rugby and all that mattered was winning, as Biggar candidly assessed after the match: "Relieved is probably the right word, and one that has been chucked around the changing room," he said. "If we are calling a spade a spade we were pretty terrible in the first 40 minutes. We have to count ourselves a bit lucky, but if you want my honest opinion I couldn't care less. We are in a World Cup semi-final. What you have got is a group of guys desperate to achieve and who are prepared to dig deep. We've trained incredibly hard for moments like today. The coaches know they are lucky they have a squad of players here who will dig as deep as anyone in the tournament. Looking at the quality of the rugby in the other quarter-finals on Saturday we were certainly below that against France, but what we have in abundance and as much as anybody is a desire and a fight not to give in. That's something that can't be trained."

There was a strange atmosphere after the match. As the clock ticked into the final minutes, it was difficult to escape the fact that the stadium was half empty. A mix of neutral spectators and a desire to avoid the travel chaos that had been experienced the night before meant thousands of fans made for the exits before full time. A tense exchange ensued when a journalist put that to Gatland, who couldn't have cared less, after the match. No Welsh man, woman or child had left the venue, though, and celebrated wildly with their team.

Suddenly, with Wales having snatched victory from the jaws of defeat, the team was heading to Yokohama, not Heathrow.

11

Springbok Despair

"I'm still proud to pull this jersey on."
Alun Wyn Jones

The day after the quarter-final the Wales bandwagon was on the move again, I was travelling from Yukuhashi to Tokyo, and the six-hour train journey would provide plenty of time for reflection.

Overnight, a picture of referee Jaco Peyper had surfaced, in which he was posing with a group of Wales fans and pretending to elbow one of them in the face, mimicking the action that resulted in him showing Sébastien Vahaamahina a red card earlier that night. Predictably, the French Rugby Federation were not too pleased and their vice president Serge Simon was among the first to demand answers. There were even ludicrous suggestions at one point that the quarter-final should be replayed.

It was a lapse in judgement on Peyper's part and it's not something referees should be getting involved with, although those questioning Peyper's impartiality were taking the whole episode a step too far. Nonetheless, Peyper was stood down for the semi-final matches and later apologised for the picture, admitting it was inappropriate.

The Wales team were back at the huge New Otani Hotel, where they had stayed in the week leading up to the Australia game. Upon the squad's arrival in Tokyo, Warren Gatland decided to hold the press conference. This was pretty unusual as Gatland is only obliged to do the team announcement and post-match press conferences.

He'd begun to show signs of his fiery old self in recent weeks and myself and the other journalists began speculating as to what his motives were. Usually, if a head coach makes an unscheduled appearance in front of the media, he's not doing it because he misses us, he's doing it because he has something to get off his chest and, usually with Gatland, if he has something to say, it's worth keeping both ears open.

Much to our dismay, however, no verbal grenades were launched, and the press conference was relatively low key. Maybe he did miss us after all! It was, however, confirmed that Josh Navidi's tournament was over. He'd suffered a grade two hamstring tear in the win over France and would be out of action for a number of weeks.

Gatland didn't let on exactly what their plans were in terms of a replacement, but he did drop hints: "Josh is no good so he'll be ruled out," said Gatland. "We'll be looking to bring in a replacement tomorrow but we've just got to go through that process, go through World Rugby at the moment and send some stuff through to them. Given that we've got six back-rowers and we've got five fit at the moment, we've been a little bit short of numbers in the backs, so it probably will be a back who comes out as a replacement. It's disappointing for him. Hopefully we will keep him out here. Obviously he loses his accreditation, but since he's gone so far in the tournament it will be nice for him to stay out for the next couple of weeks. We're just going through that with him. It's very disappointing for him as he's been very influential and important for us in the last year. It's

109

disappointing to have a player ruled out, but in saying that these games are so physical and to have only one player ruled out at this stage is a real positive for us."

As Gatland alluded to, Navidi stayed out in Japan for the remainder of the tournament but, having lost his accreditation, he was essentially a guest of the WRU for the remainder of the trip. He could stay in the team hotel but the Union had to pay for his room, and losing his accreditation meant restricting his access to team areas on matchdays but at least he was still around to soak up the final weeks of the tournament.

The real newsy stuff to latch onto from a journalist's point of view was the fact Wales were due to call up a replacement and a back was the logical choice. My first instinct was that it had to be Ospreys centre Scott Williams. I thought he was desperately unlucky to miss out in the first place, given his talent and experience, though there were concerns over his back problems. Wales had two banged-up centres and Williams could slot in there and do a job with no problems at all. At the end of the day, he'd already played at two World Cups so it would be nothing new to him.

The other option was for Cardiff Blues flier Owen Lane to get the call-up and have George North covering the midfield. Both had their merits but my hot take at the time was that Williams was the better option. Later that night I decided to test the waters and see if anyone could shed some light on who might be coming out to Japan.

Within minutes of sending my first message, a reply came back saying that Owen Lane had already left. Minutes later a second source confirmed it. Within 20 minutes of sending my first message, the story was written and up on *WalesOnline*. That's the beauty of online journalism.

Sure enough, the following day, the news was confirmed. Owen Lane had joined the squad in Japan. In reaction to the story I'd written, many fans were calling for Lane to be thrown straight into the clash against South Africa, deeming him the spark that they perceived to have been lacking in recent weeks. This was misplaced. Lane had crossed multiple time zones and had touched down in Japan on Tuesday, October 22 after a 12-hour flight from London. He was never going to be ready to face the Springboks in five days. He barely took part in training until the day the team was announced to face South Africa, it was always going to come too soon for him.

The day Lane arrived in Japan, the media interviewed Ross Moriarty. After the game he'd had in Ōita, this was always going to be pretty colourful. Shortly after arriving on the field, he'd received that yellow card which could very well have been a red on another day. He was brilliantly candid as he revealed what was going through his head as he awaited his punishment:

"As soon as I realised I had hit him in the chin – I thought I'd hit him in the shoulder – I thought: 'F***'. Excuse my language!" Said Moriarty. "I was thinking to myself: 'If he gives me a red card this is the end of me'. I was just thinking, 'please, please don't be a red'. I knew how bad that would be for the team. I've been in that situation before and it's not a nice feeling. I never go into a game intending to do anything that would get me a card or put the team at any risk of not winning."

Luckily, the back-rower went from fearing that he'd ended his Wales career to being the hero when he dived over for the winning try, he was similarly candid on that incident too: "I was running towards the ball and just thinking 'I can't mess this up'. I didn't even want to reach out in case someone came from nowhere and kicked the ball out of my hands," he laughed. "So I just landed on my head first and got the ball under my chest to make sure no one could come in and get it. That was slow-motion from myself, but it was a great scrum effort by the boys, a great rip by Tomos. Tips said he didn't know how he didn't score it. To be honest, I was thinking, 'Christ, he's basically over the line, now someone has to do it'. It ended up being me but it could have been any of us. It was probably the easiest try I've ever scored but probably the most nervous I've been scoring one."

It was another of my favourite interviews on the trip. We had the classic zero to hero narrative to form the basis of the story and then a colourful character in Moriarty to put some meat on the bones, but the day would soon take a more sombre turn. I got word that at around 6:00pm that night, the WRU were going to reveal news that we'd been expecting to break for days.

During a training session in Ōita before the France game, certain members of the media were pulled aside and made aware that Robin McBryde's mother, Diana, had passed away and he'd received the news earlier in the week. We were then asked if we would allow the Union to release the story on their terms or, more importantly, on McBryde's terms. There was never any question that the travelling hacks would fully respect these wishes.

There was a personal element to this that was much bigger than sport. When the news came out, the WRU released the following statement from McBryde:

'I have received great support from the team and management out here and with the support from my family back home it allows me to remain in Japan. My mother was my biggest fan and as with any parent, she would want the best for me, so I know I am where she would want me to be. I would like to take this opportunity to thank everyone in Ward Cybi, Ysbyty Gwynedd, for the fantastic care and attention my mother received.'

There was also a short message from Gatland, who extended the heart-felt condolences of the squad, backroom staff and WRU to McBryde and his family.

McBryde is somebody who is well-respected among those of us who covered the team regularly and that was only elevated by the way in which he carried himself during what must have been a deeply difficult time. Nobody would have batted an eyelid had he decided to leave Japan to be with his family. The fact that he wanted to stay and finish the job spoke volumes of his character.

The following day, Owen Lane was presented with his Rugby World Cup cap by none other than Prince Charles. This may seem a little random, however, the Prince of Wales was in Tokyo for the enthronement of Japan's new Emperor Naruhito. The city was awash with VIPs and royalty from countries all over the world.

The event had to be factored into Wales' movements as their hotel was being used for a number of functions throughout the week. The accommodation was crawling with security guards and roads around the hotel were closed at certain times of the day. This all had to be negotiated as they travelled to and from training on their team buses.

Prince Charles was a special guest at the Prince Chichibu Stadium during the build-up to the South Africa game, where he presented Lane with his cap in the sunshine. He conversed with the players, management team and WRU hierarchy whilst at the training session: "It was great," said team manager Alan Phillips. "These offers don't come very often. I have met him a few times over the years when we have won Six Nations Grand Slams and different things, and his two boys follow the rugby. It's just great. I was a bit cheeky this morning and asked him would he present a cap to Owen, and he said he would be absolutely delighted. Every time you meet him, you are impressed by him as a person. He is very humble, a quiet man and nice company."

Later that day came the media access to training and, of course, eyes were trained on Jonathan Davies. He was doing the same thing he'd done in the build-up to the France game: plenty of bounding work and landing on one leg to test the knee out. I was still getting mountains of messages asking what his situation was, but it was difficult to tell if he'd made any progress at all because we were simply seeing the same things.

Elsewhere in the session, though, I spotted an unusual face. Warren Gatland's son, Bryn, was out there passing a ball around and getting involved in the session. This was particularly peculiar and made me a little suspicious, especially after what had happened with Davies the previous week. I feared it may be a way of making us all look at Bryn and get excited about that story whilst hoping we didn't spot something else, like a key player being absent.

As it turned out, Bryn, who had arrived in Japan to support his father, was returning from a horror foot injury he'd suffered whilst playing for the Highlanders against the Sunwolves on the very ground where Wales were training. He was on the road to recovery and this was the first time he'd laced up his boots since having surgery.

Wales' day off that week was a particularly hectic one for me. I'd interviewed Bryan Habana in the morning, met up with Mike Phillips to work on his column and filmed a video insert for the *WalesOnline* daily show. I'd then headed over to the team hotel to film another video insert with Wales' team photographer, Ben Evans, to discuss his favourite pictures of the tournament so far, and by the time I'd travelled from place to place and written everything up, sent all the video files back, it didn't leave much time for dinner before bed. Team announcement days are busy at the best of times and I needed some sleep.

Then my phone pinged with a message from my Cardiff HQ: 'What's wrong with Liam Williams?' It read. To my knowledge, there was nothing wrong with him. I'd seen him at training just yesterday and the players were on a day off. 'We're hearing he's out of the semi-final,' came the follow-up message. Suddenly alarm bells start ringing. Had I actually seen him in training that day? I was sure I had but what if Bryn Gatland was a distraction tactic and I'd missed something.

Luckily, I was at those sessions to get footage for our website so I furiously went through the tapes to see if I could spot Williams, and there he was. I hadn't missed anything. Before I'd gone to bed that night, my colleague Mark Orders had got the story that Williams was out of the semi-final. It later transpired that he'd suffered a nasty ankle injury after the cameras had departed the training ground the day before.

Not only was he out of the semi-final, he was out of the tournament. It was at this point that I started to fear that the tournament was catching up with Wales. More specifically, the way in which they had to grind out victories over Fiji and France was taking their toll and injuries were mounting. In the backline, Williams was gone, North was carrying an ankle knock, Davies' knee was a huge concern, Parkes wasn't fully fit, Adams still had strapping on the leg he'd injured against Fiji, and Biggar had suffered two concussions.

That week a journalist asked Parkes: "Rugby players are never 100% fit, but where do you feel you're at right now?" Parkes replied, "About 99." He accompanied it with a wry smile that told us all he'd upped the figure slightly.

I didn't see similar injury concerns in the other teams that were left in the tournament. Wales were by far the gutsiest group around but this was going to be a big ask. South Africa were looking good and Wales would always have a mountain to climb if they were going to reach the final. They now stood at the foot of Everest.

The news about Williams was confirmed the following day when Wales announced their team to face the Springboks.

On a positive note, Leigh Halfpenny was by no means a bad replacement and, once again, Jonathan Davies was named in the starting side.

"Liam is undoubtedly a big loss from an attacking perspective and what he has achieved in the game in the last year or so," said Gatland. "But bringing in the experience of someone like Leigh Halfpenny gives us a different element. He is defensively probably the best full-back in the world in terms of his aerial game and coverage defensively. We had a long debate about whether we started Leigh in the first place and potentially move Liam to the wing. There was a long discussion about that so Leigh was probably unlucky he was not in the team in the first place. We are disappointed for a world-class player like Liam but we are happy bringing in someone with the experience of Leigh. It is a change but we don't think that we are weakening the side in any way with the changes we have made."

Throughout the week, I'd sensed more and more people starting to write Wales' chances off. I preferred it that way, to be totally honest. I've consistently aired my view that I think, under Gatland, Wales have traditionally been a side who are more dangerous when they are the underdogs. They'd discovered a newfound comfort in being favourites as well, but I think they still relished the underdog tag. So I put it to the Wales boss.

"If they continue to do that over the next couple of days that would be brilliant, please continue to do that as it does get us up when people write us off," he replied. "I can't understand why people would write us off when our record against South Africa has been pretty good in the last four or five years. That speaks for itself.

"Going into Sunday's game it is going to be a tight game and we saw that the first half in South Africa vs Japan was a tight game. It will probably be a kicking fest, they kicked 30 times against Japan so we just have got to handle their game. It won't be the prettiest game in the world, it will be a tight Test match with probably teams playing for territory depending on what the weather is like. The ball will go in the air and we have got to be able to handle that and we have got to be able to handle our game as well."

After the press conference, myself and two other journalists who had been following Wales everywhere they went for the last few years were given the opportunity to interview Jonathan Davies. We hot-footed it over to the other side of the hotel and up a lift to the 16th floor, where the team room was located, and sat around a coffee table just outside it.

Davies emerged, no press officer present, and off we went into the interview. At this point, I still had doubts in my mind over his fitness based on what I'd seen but the very fact that we were given access to him offered some reassurance in my mind that the management must be confident. I'd interviewed Davies one-on-one before and, in an intimate setting, he is happy to open up.

We covered it all. We established a timeline of events, heard how a complication with Japanese radiographers delayed him getting the results of his scan as they were sent back to the UK to be read and how he feared he'd reinjured his anterior cruciate ligament. He thought his World Cup was over but what struck me was the thought-process that he went through when he pulled out of the quarter-final.

"Everyone had worked too hard for me to go into the game selfishly just to play in a quarter-final," he said. "I trained on the Friday and it was a bit sore towards the end and on the day of the 'captain's run' it reacted, was a bit swollen, and wasn't great when I was warming up. I stopped in the team run. I didn't even get going really. It was a case of ice up and compression for the next 24 hours to see if the swelling would go down. On the morning of the game me and Prav (Mathema) did a few drills to see if I could get up and running, but I could tell I wasn't right. Prav could see it as well. We made a decision that it was probably best for the team if I didn't play."

You've got to remember that Davies missed the 2015 World Cup through injury and, at the age of 31, is probably in the midst of his final global gathering. I thought it was incredibly impressive to have the selflessness to make that decision, knowing deep down that he wasn't right and would be putting the team at risk.

After interviewing Davies, we had to race out to Yokohama Stadium to get there in time to watch Wales train for 15 minutes. All four teams trained there on the Friday, and because England were facing New Zealand there the day before the Wales game, Gatland's side wouldn't get the chance to have their 'captain's run' at the venue.

When we got to the stadium, the pitch was in a state. It had been raining heavily all day and through the previous night. Straight away, I fired off messages to World Rugby and the WRU to get their take on the situation. A huge puddle stretched through one of the 22-metre areas and towards the 10-metre line. Players had to hop through another big puddle on the touchline to get to the surface and there was plenty of splashing all over the pitch as players ran through standing water that wasn't visible from my vantage point in the stand.

At first, I had genuine fears that the games would have to be moved or postponed, but the message came back from World Rugby to say they were confident in the drainage system at the ground. Fair enough, I thought. I disappeared into the press room after the access to training ended and worked there for a few hours. By the time I left the ground, the pitch was pretty much clear. Some drainage system.

Just like the previous weekend, I went to watch England's game, this time against New Zealand in the semi-final. Wales would end up playing one of the two sides in whatever match, so I deemed it to be a worthwhile trip.

England were, once again, mightily impressive. It was one of the greatest England performances I'd ever seen. Nobody saw it coming. They didn't just beat New Zealand, they pummelled the two-time defending champions and made them look ordinary. It finished 19-7 to England, and that scoreline flattered the All Blacks. It was ominous stuff.

The next day I got to the stadium early, having already slurped a now customary pint of coffee beforehand, and did my usual Facebook Live for the *WalesOnline* page. As I took my seat in the press box, I wasn't as confident in Wales' chances as I had been in previous weeks, months and years. I thought it would be one of Gatland's greatest achievements if he could get this group of players through the match. They would have to do it on raw emotion and desire. If he was able to conjure up enough fire inside them to beat the Springboks, it would eclipse much of what he had done in his previous 12 years.

The first half was pretty forgettable. Gatland had called it in the week. It was a kickfest. It was like being at Wimbledon's Centre Court, watching the ball ping back and forth, but whenever it remained on the ground long enough for a few phases to break out, it always felt like the Springboks were the aggressors even when they didn't have the ball.

Wales were struggling to make inroads anywhere and were losing the collisions on the gainline, which is normally a good indicator of which team is on top. Dan Biggar and Handre Pollard traded penalties throughout the first half but neither side really looked particularly threatening and the game was largely played in the air and between the two 10-metre lines.

More injuries came for Wales, though. Tomas Francis suffered a nasty-looking shoulder injury as he attempted to stop Duane Vermeulen in full flight. Minutes later it was George

North. Wales had a penalty advantage near the end of the first half and Biggar send it skyward towards North's wing. I hadn't seen the incident, but minutes before the winger's hamstring had twinged.

What was evident as North attempted to burst off the mark to get after the kick was that the muscle in the back of his leg had done more than twinge. He'd torn it. There was a collective groan as North staggered into his opposite man and made some sort of contact. Play was brought back as North punched the turf. It's never easy to watch a player go through this.

I'd seen a snapshot of what the players had put into this campaign, what they'd sacrificed, and had a decent understanding of the whole picture. I thought North had come in for some unfair criticism during the tournament. I saw a lot of people accuse him of not coming off his wing enough. It was lazy criticism and incorrect. I'd seen him venture off his wing regularly throughout the tournament, the ball just evaded him.

North was being treated as Biggar was preparing to kick at goal and the winger tried to stagger back into position, he only had one minute until half time but there was no way he could continue. He hobbled towards the sideline and a jacket was slung over his shoulder as he slumped onto the bench. Just 24 hours earlier, he'd spoken about this being one of the biggest games of his life.

When Biggar kicked Wales level in the 46th minute, there was a sense that perhaps the men in red had weathered the onslaught and could now begin to impose themselves on the game, but it never quite happened. Instead, as the game approached the hour mark, Damian de Allende crossed for South Africa, with Pollard's conversion stretching the lead out to seven.

It was a soft try to concede. Biggar didn't need to be told that he was shrugged off too easily and other players were carried over the line but it was a sign that South Africa's power was beginning to tell. Knowing they were in serious danger of being booted out of the competition, Wales came back hard and really took control of the game. They battered away at the Springbok line but couldn't find a way through. They were awarded a very kickable penalty deep in the South Africa 22 and skipper Alun Wyn Jones opted for the scrum. If Wales failed to score from this position, it was game over.

Ross Moriarty worked wonders at the back to feed Tomos Williams, who sent it to Josh Adams, via Jonathan Davies, for a simple run in down the blind side. The gamble had paid off. With Rhys Patchell now on for Dan Biggar, Halfpenny kicked at goal and slotted it nervelessly to bring the scores level. From that point, Wales really got on the front foot and were the ones in the ascendency heading into the final minutes.

Then, as the game hung in the balance, there was a penalty at a breakdown in the Springbok half that gave Rassie Erasmus' side field position and then Jérôme Garcès, who in my opinion hadn't had the greatest night either way, penalised Rhys Carre for dragging a maul down.

Replays showed that Carre fell over a South Africa body that was already on the floor but that decision decided the outcome of the match. Pollard hadn't looked like missing all afternoon and kicked South Africa three points in front with four minutes remaining. Wales barely got a sniff of the ball again and South Africa closed the game out to win 19-16.

My job at these matches was to latch onto the things that fans back at home weren't able to see on TV and provide the colour to go with it.

When Pollard booted the ball off the field to end the game, it was noticeable that not a single Welsh player fell straight to the floor, as players usually do in this scenario. They all just stood there and stared into nothingness. Alun Wyn Jones just stood there, looking at the ground and his team-mates did the same. It was peculiar but perhaps symbolic of this group of players who'd refused to throw in the towel.

Wales and Gatland took some heat for the way they had performed. They engaged in a kicking battle and had appeared to take the Springboks on at their own game. Some felt Wales could have been more ambitious and expansive in the way they played. Initially, Wales had looked threatening a little wider, with North in particular getting some joy, but for me, the tournament had caught up with them and, when your body gets tired, you simplify things, you become more inclined to stick it up your jumper rather than look for space. You lose the desire to be creative and I think that's what we saw. Also, it's easy to say Wales should have thrown the ball around but they'd lost their creative spark in Liam Williams before the game and then had a centre in Owen Watkin playing on the wing for half of it.

I felt as though the way Wales were forced to win the matches against Fiji and France had taken their toll and the performance against South Africa was evidence of that. The frustration came in the fact that, despite all of that, Wales still had a chance to win the game. Gatland refused to admit that he harboured any regrets.

"I'm very disappointed but incredibly proud of what this group of players has done at this World Cup," said Gatland after the match. "We can hold our heads high and leave Japan with a lot of respect. We've got another game to go, we play the All Blacks. My first game in charge was against England and the dream was for it to be my last game, but it's not to be. This is a great group of players that we've been involved with, and coaches. We need to recover well over the next couple of days and start preparing for the All Blacks. We're really disappointed about tonight and not being in the final but we've got to be proud of ourselves. Robin McBryde said in the changing room afterwards, after all the hard work we've done and what this group of players and coaches have achieved, Friday will be our last time together. So we're going to make sure we enjoy this week."

The mixed zone afterwards was an uncomfortable place to be. As always, the various UK journalists there all split up to make sure we caught as many of the players coming through as we could. Before I'd given any thought to what I might ask, Hadleigh Parkes was stood in front of me. I threw up some pretty straightforward questions and he threw back some pretty expected answers. It's tough to know how to phrase questions in that situation. There's very little the players can say so soon after such disappointment. At that point, they haven't fully comprehended the disappointment.

In his interview in the immediate aftermath Alun Wyn Jones mustered: "It wasn't our day but I'm still proud to pull this jersey on and represent all the people in red in the stadium." He repeated the message in the changing room afterwards.

That night I finished work at around 2:00am in a communal area on the second floor of my hotel. The staff had turned the lights off and I couldn't locate the switch so I was in the pitch black filing my final words back to the desk in Cardiff before shutting the laptop down.

It was as if I'd been on a hamster wheel for the last two months and I'd just stepped off it, so goodness only knows how the players must have been feeling at that point. The life had been sucked out of the tour but there was still the small matter of a game against the All Blacks with just five days to prepare.

12

A Game Nobody Wants

"Steve Tew made a joke that both teams should have a boat race and we could settle it that way!"
Warren Gatland

Wales took the Monday off. Goodness knows they needed it. They had to deal with the emotional scars as well as the physical ones but had little time to wallow in the disappointment of what had happened over the weekend.

Their punishment for losing the semi-final to South Africa? A date with the back-to-back defending champions who'd just been embarrassed – by their standards – by England. The All Blacks were wounded and they lay in wait with an extra day's rest. Talk about rubbing salt into the wound.

In the immediate aftermath of the defeat to the Springboks, there had been some admirable talk of wanting to fight until the bitter end and beat New Zealand, something no Welsh side had managed since 1953, but if that was going to happen, Wales were going to have to move on pretty swiftly because the All Blacks were not going to be in the mood for showing mercy.

Wales had to assess the shape of their battered squad. Gatland and his lieutenants would have to come up with a 23 that could compete with New Zealand without pushing certain players too hard in what was, essentially, the game nobody wanted to play in.

First, though, there was time for a little reflection. Robin McBryde was put in front of the media early in the week. It was not going to be an easy press conference. Part of me wondered whether he might now take the opportunity to fly back to Wales given there was nothing of any great value to play for. McBryde wasn't having any of that. He was staying in Japan until the job was finished: "I'm very fortunate to be surrounded by strong women in my life. Both my wife and my sisters," he said as he held back the tears. "With their support I've been able to stay out here and just focus on the work. Obviously the players and the management out here have made it a lot easier for me. It's been a difficult time but I've been able to enjoy it as well."

Talking about rugby after that question was asked felt a little bit pointless to me but McBryde seemed happy enough to go there, cracking jokes as he was asked if this All Blacks side were vulnerable. He intimated that this game was only of real value to him because of the fact they were playing Steve Hansen's side before adding: "It would be good to get one over on Steve ... He's miserable as hell isn't he! I can say that because I know him pretty well."

Despite the jokes, there was no getting away from the fact that this coaching team, who had been together for so many years under Gatland were in their final days as a unit. That was strange but then, as McBryde pointed out, it had been that way from the start: "Unfortunately, it's been a bit different right from the word go when Rob went. I just hope that the boys go out there and show what they can do. The game against South Africa was a tense affair, quite a tight game really. I think it will be the complete opposite on Friday night. There will be two teams going out there and wanting to show their skills. Hopefully it will be a good advert for rugby as well. We've had a fantastic time in Japan and people will be turning up to watch that game, hoping to see some great tries."

Those few quotes set the tone for the week. The pressure was off now and, for the first time in months, players could go out and play with a freedom that hadn't been afforded to them previously. Up until that point, I'd been dreading the game but it started to change my attitude towards it. That being said, I always questioned the relevance of it.

Given the collisions in modern day rugby, the speed of the game and the amount of injuries that are now being suffered, I feel as though World Rugby need to take a long hard look at the bronze medal match. Wales had played six Test matches in just under five weeks and were now being asked to play against the All Blacks on a five-day turnaround. The demand that sort of schedule places on players is incredible.

The week was set to fly by as a day after speaking to McBryde, Gatland had to name his team having barely conducted a training session. As expected, there were a few changes, nine in all to the side that started the semi-final and Owen Lane was one of them as he was pencilled in to make his Rugby World Cup debut just a week after arriving in Japan.

At first I was surprised to see some familiar names starting. Jonathan Davies, who'd been battling that serious knee injury, was in his usual No.13 shirt, Alun Wyn Jones, who'd been an absolute warrior throughout the campaign was also starting, as was Ken Owens. Nobody would have begrudged these players a rest, but they were starting. I noticed there was a bit of flak flying Gatland's way on social media for their selections as well, but then when I began to read between the lines of what was being said that week, I got the impression that little was going to come between those players and this game.

Given their age profiles, this was their last chance to play at a Rugby World Cup. I don't think they wanted to let that pass them by. When I asked Alun Wyn Jones about it afterwards, he replied: "I've started it [this journey] so I'm going to finish it. Everyone has got a few niggles. There are a few guys who are unfortunately injured and can't be selected, but everyone was champing at the bit to play in this one, to finish it off, because it's the last one we have."

Before we got to speak to the captain, we first had Gatland's final pre-game press conference as Wales boss. I wondered if he shared my fears that this game seemed to put the players in harm's way for the sake of it.

"It's the last game you want to be involved in, but it's been on the calendar and everyone has known about it," said Gatland. "I think Steve Tew [NZRU CEO] made a joke to Martyn Phillips [WRU CEO] that both teams should have a boat race and we could settle it that way! I can see the relevance in that! When you put the disappointment behind you, you think about the chance to play the All Blacks and that gets you excited. Hopefully as coaches we've put the disappointment of the last 48 hours behind us and can start getting excited for the next 24. It's the same for the group of players. We want to go out, perform well, and be positive about the way we play."

In the aftermath of the defeat to South Africa, Gatland had made a comment about England that had irked Eddie Jones and sparked a relatively unpleasant if not entirely expected verbal joust: "We've seen in previous World Cups, sometimes teams play their final in semi-finals and don't always turn up in the final." He said. "It will be interesting to see how England are next week." True to form, Jones responded with: "Can you just send my best wishes to Warren to make sure he enjoys the third and fourth place play-off."

The Wales boss was given the chance to set the record straight in his press conference after announcing his team for the bronze medal match: "I was reflecting on the experiences I've seen in the past," said Gatland. "I was thinking about 2011 and the All Blacks. They had a big game against Australia in the semi-final and they maybe looked at that as their final. They played France in the final and it was probably a game they thought they could potentially win comfortably. It ended up being a very tight game. It was just observations I'd made of the past. I thought England were excellent against the All Blacks – it was the best I've seen England play in the last 10 years. I thought they were outstanding. I wish them all the best. There are a lot of players there who I've been fortunate to have had personal contact with through the Lions and I want to wish them all the best."

There was more bad news to pass on as far as injuries were concerned as well. Aaron Wainwright, who'd thrived on the biggest stage of his young career had also suffered a hamstring injury ruling him out of the All Blacks clash, and Leigh Halfpenny was unavailable having failed a head injury assessment after the match. Meanwhile, Liam Williams had already returned to have surgery on his ankle and was expected to be out for three months. The tournament had really taken its toll on the players and the injury list had suddenly grown significantly in a short space of time.

After Gatland had finished his press conference, the writers sat down to conduct an interview with captain Alun Wyn Jones, that was to be embargoed until 10:00pm that night.

Usually at the World Cup, Jones sat next to Gatland on the top table and, because most of the questions are directed at the head coach, the second row was mainly an observer. This sit down was a good chance to get into the nitty gritty of where his head was at.

Those who cover Wales regularly know that as long as there is a game to be played, Jones does not want to talk about his future and any attempt to take the conversation there will be shut down with haste. Unfortunately, one French journalist who was covering the press conference was not aware of this. Even worse, he mistakenly thought Jones had announced he'd be retiring after the match, which was not the case. He proceeded to ask the Wales captain if the All Blacks were the best team to play in your final game.

An awkward exchange ensued as Wales' press officer got involved to set the record straight and move the interview along as Jones went on to admit this was probably his last shot at a World Cup with Wales: "You can be selfish at times, make no bones about it I think am one of the eight to 10 [players] who aren't going to have another World Cup," he said. "From a selfish point of view I will acknowledge that and that's probably why this one meant so much. It is what it is, we have another game and a lot of the guys here will have another opportunity. I will be right behind them in whatever guise I have when that time comes around."

Read between the lines. Do you think he didn't want to be involved in this game? Interviewing the Wales skipper is always an interesting experience and, after pointing out that he still had some miles left in the tank, we concluded. As he left the huddle, he nodded towards the French journalist and quipped: "I'll see you in February."

All tournament long, the welcome all visitors, not just the players, had received in Japan was superb, but I couldn't escape the feeling that the tournament had got a little bit lost in the hustle and bustle of Tokyo. Everywhere else we'd been, it felt like you were at the heart of the tournament because it was consuming the city. If anything, though, Tokyo was consuming the tournament.

Nonetheless, that night as I was paying for my dinner in a restaurant, the waiter asked where I was from. I managed to explain that I was from Wales. His face lit up and he got excited, telling me about how much he was enjoying the tournament. As I turned to leave, he said to me: "You are from Wales, that means we are on the same team." He was clearly one of the vast amount of locals that had taken to Wales as their second team and was now fully behind them after Japan had exited the tournament. That exchange summed up the people of Japan and how hospitable and welcoming they had been.

The next day, the squad did their 'captain's run' at the training venue that was local to their hotel, rather than making the 45 minutes bus journey out to Tokyo Stadium, a venue where they had already played. Dan Biggar, who'd been named on the bench to face the All Blacks with Patchell starting, had decided not to make the trip out to the stadium so Rhys Patchell, Leigh Halfpenny and Hallam Amos all went for some kicking practise. It was good to see Halfpenny running around out on the pitch after his recent history with concussions.

In fact, it was good to see him acquit himself so well in the semi-final against South Africa. I'd interviewed Halfpenny twice in the year leading up to the World Cup. The first time we spoke about his battle with concussion after the Samu Kerevi incident in 2018, while the second time focused on how his 2015 tournament was ended before it started by a knee injury in the final warm up match against Italy. We joked that one day I might interview him about something positive, but with all the anecdotes I picked up from those interviews in the back of my mind, it was good to see him perform well on that stage.

The press conference that followed the session, with Neil Jenkins, Patchell and Amos, was dominated by talk of Gatland and his final game in charge of Wales. It was the eloquent Patchell that put it best for me: "The biggest thing you find with Warren is that he has an uncanny ability to work out what people need," he said. "Whether somebody needs an arm around the shoulder, needs their tyres pumped up or if someone needs a pin to take a bit out of them to give them a bit of a rocket for the weekend. He's been great for me over the past couple of years when I've been a bit more involved with the national squad. Hopefully he carries on with the success he's had here wherever he goes but he certainly deserves that."

A little over 24 hours later and it was time for one final outing in Japan. If the South Africa game felt like one too far, goodness knows what was going to happen here. A lot was made about it being the final game for Gatland and his coaching team but it was also going to be Steve Hansen's last game in charge of the All Blacks, ending a 15-year association with the side as an assistant and then head coach.

Captain Kieran Read was also retiring from international rugby, as was the much-liked Ben Smith. The men in black had plenty of motivation, so when prop Joe Moody was running in a try from 22 metres out and Beauden Barrett was slicing through some weak Welsh defence to add another after 13 minutes, you feared the worst.

To Wales' credit, though, they got into the game and scored a lovely try of their own just minutes later, with Hallam Amos breaking onto a zipped miss pass from Rhys Patchell, that beat Ben Smith to send the Wales full-back over. Patchell added a penalty and Wales were right in the game and playing some decent stuff, but just before the break they conceded two incredibly soft Ben Smith tries, which came as hammer blows. Gatland's side hadn't made many mistakes but the All Blacks punished them ruthlessly.

Though there wasn't a great deal of control, Patchell was moving nicely and showing some nice touches. He appeared a totally different player to the one who arrived in Wales camp all those months ago, totally devoid of confidence. It was pleasing to see how far he'd come, but the game was getting away from Wales. Ryan Crotty added another just after the break and killed the game off.

As we'd been promised during the week, it was an entertaining game. Just before the hour mark, Wales skipper Alun Wyn Jones was replaced by Jake Ball. As Jones approached the touchline, everyone who was sat on the Welsh bench and in the stand rose to their feet to applaud him. It was a pretty touching moment but it was fitting. Jones would finish the tournament as the top tackler by a distance, which tells you everything you need to know about his desire and commitment to the cause.

Meanwhile, on the field, Josh Adams managed to burrow his way over for his most unglamorous try of the competition. He'd been looking for the ball all night and was desperate to get that seventh try. It saw him set a Welsh record for tries scored at a single World Cup, eclipsing Shane Williams' tally from 2007. It also meant he ended the tournament as the top try-scorer.

Kiwi Richie Mo'unga added a late score to bring a rip-roaring bronze medal match to a close. New Zealand won 40-17. The 1987 effort remained Wales' best finish at a World Cup.

If he isn't already on the touchline by the time the final whistle blows, it normally doesn't take long for Warren Gatland to appear. First and foremost he is usually there to greet his players but he also has media commitments to fulfil, but on this occasion he was nowhere to be seen.

Players had shaken hands and the occasion was winding down as tournament organisers set up a stage for the All Blacks to collect their bronze medals. Alun Wyn Jones had done his post-match interview, Kieran Read had done his and Steve Hansen was in the middle of his but still Gatland was nowhere to be seen. Attack coach Stephen Jones, the late addition to the setup, had appeared on the touchline but McBryde, Edwards and Gatland were still absent.

At this point, Wales' media manager is scurrying around the pitch desperately trying to find Gatland to usher him towards the backdrop and TV crew. He disappears into the tunnel. McBryde and Edwards are now on the touchline and suddenly Gatland and the press officer emerge from the bowels of the stadium and out onto the pitch. Quite where he was and what he was doing was anyone's guess. Had he and his coaching team shared a quiet moment in the dressing room at full time? Only they will know.

There were lovely scenes on the pitch after the match as the likes of Dan Biggar, Alun Wyn Jones, Jake Ball and Ken Owens went to get their young children from the stands and let them roam on the pitch. Players and coaches from both sides caught up and unwound after months of hard work.

After the All Blacks had received their medals, every Wales player made their way to the centre of the pitch to bow to all four stands, as they had done all tour. Only this time they were joined by every member of management and the backroom staff to say 'thank you' and 'goodbye' to their hosts.

When he arrived in the post-match press conference, Gatland had the look of a man who had perhaps shed a few tears just moments earlier. He insisted, however, that the day was not as emotional as some might have expected, having already been through a similar experience with his final game in Cardiff months earlier.

"It was about the players. Shaun Edwards spoke to the group and so did Robin McBryde. Alan Phillips had a few words as well," said Gatland. "There wasn't a lot to be said. We spoke about the opportunity to go out and play a pretty good side. We spoke about how disappointed we were that we weren't in the final but, to play the All Blacks, at least that was a game that you could look forward to. I think I've already gone through that process of knowing it was my last game and not trying to get too emotional about it. I came to the realisation a while ago. I'd prepared myself for it.

He added: "I really hope – for what we've achieved in the last 12 years and we feel like we've put some respect back into Wales as an international team – the new coaches come in and continue to build on that. After what we've done and achieved, it would break my heart of Wales went back into the doldrums."

That was a pretty emotive line for someone like Gatland, probably as emotive as I'd seen from him for a long time. There was some light relief as one journalist pointed out that his next match would see him coach against Wales for the Barbarians, which brought a smile to faces.

I managed to throw one last question at Gatland, before he departed the scene, to ask what his advice for Wayne Pivac would be. I was expecting a little bit more banter but I got the total opposite: "I think what we've done and created is that we've always spoken about how important family is," he said. "It's not about the rugby, it's about putting family first. We're very lucky and very privileged to do what we do. If things are right at home for the players and you make their home life as easy as you possibly can. It's not a normal job. It's weekends, public holidays, Christmas and all that. If things are right at home, then I know that I get a better product on the training ground and the rugby field."

With that he was gone. Gatland had fulfilled his final media duty as Wales head coach, after 12 long years. As I stood up and started chatting to the other journalists about who was going to type up which section of the quotes – this is done to save us all typing out 12 minutes or so of quotes, instead four of us will do three minutes each and send it around, for example – I felt a presence behind me. It was Alun Wyn Jones, who'd arrived at the press conference in his pants. He thanked myself and the other handful of journalists who'd followed Wales every step of the way in Japan and shook our hands. A classy touch.

In the mixed zone, there was a lot of talk of the future and life after Gatland. A number of young players came through, who themselves would be tasked with shaping the future of the national squad under Pivac. It was good to hear them talk of the responsibility they felt now and, again, Patchell put it best: "There are a group of younger boys here who have had a taste of how things should be in terms of the standards that we set and the expectations, coming to work every Monday with a good attitude to get better and being stubborn about that," he said. "That's down to us. He's [Gatland] done his bit. Now it's down to the squad and the new set of coaches to pick that up and run as far and as fast and as hard as we can with it. We'll see where that takes us."

James Davies was a little punchier, stating that "fourth wasn't good enough" and hoped players would remember the feeling for four years time. As the final few players filtered through the mixed zone in Tokyo Stadium, their 'official' Rugby World Cup was over and that was the last we saw of them. Due to the tight turnaround since the semi-final I got the impression they hadn't fully let their hair down, totally relaxed and enjoyed the moment together, so they now had 48 hours in which they could do just that or whatever they pleased.

The following day, South Africa were crowned champions of the world, beating a pretty lacklustre England side 32-12. It appeared Gatland was right and England had struggled to get themselves back to the same levels they reached in the semi-final. Eddie Jones conceded afterwards that his side might have struggled with an emotional hangover from the New Zealand victory.

On the Sunday, at the World Rugby Awards Dinner, Warren Gatland missed out on Coach of the Year to Rassie Erasmus and Alun Wyn Jones was beaten to Player of the Year by Pieter-Steph du Toit. After the Springboks had just won the World Cup, it came as a surprise to nobody.

The squad left Japan at around 2:00am on Monday morning and that was it. After years of planning and months of blood, sweat and tears in the build-up, seven weeks were over in a flash.

It was a strange moment for the players. Six months previously the first players began arriving in camp to prepare for this tournament. Since then, winning the Rugby World Cup had taken over their lives. They'd lived and breathed it. Now it was all over.

Back in 2016, in that hotel in Wellington, the coaching group and WRU hierarchy had set out to have 'No Regrets' and only they will know whether they had any when they flew home from Japan. Publicly, Gatland refused to go there in the aftermath of the South Africa game and reiterated how proud he was of this group of players and the effort they had put in. It was a bitter pill to swallow because so much had gone into making this campaign a success, but ultimately Wales had fallen short at the World Cup again.

13

The Gatland Legacy

"The biggest thing I am proud of is that I think we have earned respect from the rest of the world."
Warren Gatland

When Warren Gatland took over as Wales head coach, to say the red jersey was in a dark place would be putting it lightly. Wales were not a credible threat to the best teams in the world, they were not even a concern for Six Nations rivals. Almost overnight, Gatland changed that.

Winning that 2008 Grand Slam was clearly a huge moment but mostly because it proved to the players that his methods worked. If they bought into the level of commitment that was demanded of them, they would reap the rewards. Since then, the success Wales have enjoyed has been unprecedented in the professional era and that has raised the bar.

It is no longer acceptable for Wales to win at Twickenham one weekend and capitulate to Scotland the next. The fans won't allow it and the players demand more of themselves. That mentality has come as a result of four Six Nations titles and three Grand Slams during his tenure, as well as two World Cup semi-final appearances.

"There is always an expectancy and that comes with the record that Warren had before arriving and since then he has just improved on that record," said assistant Robin McBryde. "Any team that faces a Warren Gatland side know it will be a tough challenge. Any player who has been under Warren, their values have been consistent right from the word go: family, hard work. There is an expectancy and the environment he has created in the last 12 years ... You've seen players flourish and really grow in that environment.

"Everybody is asking what sort of legacy will we leave behind? There's no better legacy than the players that are here now, the players that will be here in eight years at other World Cups. Those players and the experience that they've had, rubbing shoulders with some of these more experienced players, that's the legacy. These players know how to win. It's testament to Warren, the other coaches he brought with him, the environment, the backroom staff. These players have been given the best opportunity possible. There is a 'no-excuse' sort of environment. There's no way out. That expectancy, that pressure, is always there to win. Warren's mentality has fed down to everybody. Regardless of who we're playing, we expect to go out there and win."

As a player, Neil Jenkins was part of a Wales side that experienced some fairly dark days throughout the 1990s, but as a coach he has been part of the Wales setup under Gatland that has enjoyed unrivalled success, and as such, he believes that a simple thank-you doesn't cut it: "I've said it before, he's an incredible man not just due to his rugby intelligence and knowledge, but he's an unbelievable person," said Jenkins. "A thank-you is not enough as far as I'm concerned. For me he is a god of the game. I've been very, very lucky to be involved with him since he started in 2008. I'd like to think he's left a fantastic legacy through the results and successes he's had since 2008.

There has been the development of a lot of good players coming through and there are a lot of youngsters in the squad at this moment in time. Yes there are players who could be at their last World Cup, but there are a lot of players who will be at the next one and hopefully the one after that. Warren's knowledge and what he's done for our game is immense."

Even down to his final team selection, Gatland had one eye on the future of Welsh rugby, a future that didn't involve him. By selecting the likes of Hallam Amos, Owen Lane, Owen Watkin, Rhys Patchell, Tomos Williams and Dillon Lewis to start against the All Blacks, he was giving players who would shape the next four years of the side invaluable experience against some of the best players in the world.

"He's always had one eye on that," said Alun Wyn Jones of Gatland's decision to develop players for the future. "He is fiercely loyal, not only to players but to the country and the job. When the pressure has come on he has stuck to his guns. When you talk about change, he has been reluctant to do that at times, and it has paid off. He's had the Midas touch at times. It's a credit to him as a person – more than as a rugby coach or anything like that – that he wants to give the next regime the best chance possible. It also puts the pressure on. That expectation is always going to be there. I can see him wanting to pave the way and someone to carry on from the foundations he's set."

To sum up, Gatland altered the perception of what was acceptable in professional rugby in Wales. He has rubbed people up the wrong way at times and, even to this day, he has his detractors who take issue with the style of rugby that he employed. That will always come when you are in charge of a team for so long, but the success he has enjoyed with the side over such a long period is undeniable. There are an entire generation of fans out there who have only known a successful

Welsh national side. Those of us who were around before his tenure know how lucky they are.

What happens next is up to the coaches who take the reins but there will be hope that, having altered the psyche of Welsh rugby fans, he has changed the game in this little corner of the world forever.

"The biggest thing I am proud of is that I think we have earned respect from the rest of the world in terms of what we have achieved in the last 12 years," said Gatland out in Japan. "I am not sure it was there before that."

It's tough to argue with him.

14

Future Prospects – Future Winners?

"I've had my time but I'm jealous of any coach that is going to grab hold and work with these players."
Robin McBryde

So what now for the Wales national team? The first thing to note is that for virtually this entire crop of players, the only head coach they've ever had has been Warren Gatland, and skipper Alun Wyn Jones is the only player who made his Wales debut before Gatland took over.

This is going to be a totally new experience for a lot of them. It's both an exciting time but a daunting time. Many of these players will have to prove themselves again and may be fearing for their place in the side. Reputations should count for little moving into this new era as Pivac begins to put his stamp on things.

The winds of change may sweep through the Principality Stadium but it would be foolish if it became a gale. Pivac needs to tap into Stephen Jones in a big way in the short term. Gatland created a winning environment that enabled Wales, who have a significantly lower playing base than many of their rivals, to compete at rugby's top table.

After his call-up to replace Rob Howley, Jones experienced everything that environment and the culture had to offer. He is in a great position to be able to feed back the best bits of the Gatland regime and guide Pivac on how they need to be tweaked or improved. Neil Jenkins and Paul Stridgeon (the WRU's fitness chief) will also be able to do the same.

"I've had my time but I'm jealous of any coach that is going to grab hold and work with these players," said Robin McBryde in the final week of the tournament. "Look at the ages of some of them and the successful experiences they've had: knowing how to win games, being in tight situations and getting out of it on top. If you don't win, you're always wondering 'what's the magic recipe? What's the secret?' but those players have experienced it first hand, so they know it's down to hard work and some of those values that I've spoken about. Any coach, coming in to work with these individuals, they have to be excited. The talent there. Tomos Williams to name one who has stood out, Aaron Wainwright is another one. These are young men who have got really bright futures."

Pivac has to be true to himself and look to implement his own gameplan, methods and ideas, but he mustn't dismiss the best bits of what Gatland brought. In the last three Rugby World Cups, Wales have not been that far away. Yes, they have fallen short, but all three have been agonising. They are just a little fine tuning away from getting over that hill under Pivac.

"Warren has added a grit, perhaps, and a winning mentality. That's what sport is all about," said James Davies. "I think he has instilled that in most players that he has coached, so in fairness to him, he's done one hell of a job. He's given Wayne a good platform and Wayne is an amazing coach. I'm sure he'll have a different style of play perhaps but he'll want the attitude that the players have shown to carry through. That's probably the hardest thing for a coach to get out of players sometimes. Wayne's a brilliant man manager. He's been fantastic with us at the Scarlets and I think he will bring a style of play that will excite the fans and hopefully the players. I've loved playing under him at the Scarlets, with the open style of play. When you get it right, it's hard to stop. Hopefully the players who get selected can implement that style of play."

There are a number of unknowns heading into the future, though. The squad will have a distinctly different look and feel to it by the time we reach France in 2023. By the players' own admissions, many of them will struggle to make the next global showcase and this will be Pivac's biggest task, how he manages the transition of the squad, as a nucleus, as players edge away from the international game. From the word go, Pivac needs to identify which players are going to take him through to the next World Cup and the uncapped players that he needs to blood. He mustn't simply dispense with the old guard. Their experience and knowledge will be invaluable in bringing through the next generation of this national side.

"I forget sometimes that I'm just 23 and I've had a lot of experience at this level," Dillon Lewis said after the tournament. "I am very hard on myself and I only want to be the best I can possibly be. That's something that Warren has put in place by demanding the highest of standards. I think Welsh rugby is an exciting place to be. Look at international rugby in Wales, there are a lot of good youngsters coming through. The likes of myself, Owen Lane, Owen Watkin, Rhys Carre – he has only just broken onto the scene and has just a handful of games. It's definitely something to be excited about. I hope to be a part of it. Welsh rugby and Wales as a nation can look forward to seeing it."

Gatland has already laid the foundations. Many players who will be around for the next World Cup and maybe even the one after that have already been capped and will shape the future of the side. The likes of Rhys Carre, Elliot Dee, Dillon Lewis, Adam Beard, Aaron Wainwright, Ellis Jenkins, Tomos Williams, Jarrod Evans, Owen Watkin and Owen Lane will all have vital roles to play. Not to mention the experienced campaigners who still have another four-year cycle in them.

"I just feel like Warren has done a fantastic job of giving us boys an opportunity," said Lane after that New Zealand defeat. "Even the likes of Hallam [Amos] and a few other boys who are established are still relatively young in terms of their international careers. Yeah, we do have somewhat of a responsibility to continue where Warren left us. Hopefully Wayne [Pivac] and Stephen [Jones] – having him in training has been fantastic – can bring their own imprint and we can just build on that and achieve even better than we have in this World Cup."

This is professional sport and it's a results-based industry but Pivac must be afforded time to get things right. Gatland's 2008 Grand Slam was a freak incident, those sort of starts do not happen very often. It could take a year for players to adapt to what Pivac wants them to do, having been conditioned to do things a little differently for so long. If results don't come straight away, it should not be the time for panic.

Gatland brought a lot of success to Wales and teams now respect the red jersey when, in the past, they did not. That's a big act to follow and could be quite daunting for Pivac, but it's also a fantastic opportunity. Wales became one of the fittest sides in world rugby under Gatland but that wasn't enough to get them over the line. The key for Pivac is uncovering what was missing.

Fortunately for the incoming coach, there are a lot of younger players in the current Wales squad who are now accustomed to winning big games, they expect to come out on top every time they take the field. That mentality is invaluable.

There are also a number of exciting prospects that have come through the Welsh Premiership and regional system who've thrived for the Wales under-20s team in recent years, such as Ben Thomas at the Cardiff Blues, Dewi Lake at the Ospreys, and Ryan Conbeer at the Scarlets. Others, currently outside of Wales, like Sam Costelow at Leicester Tigers, Ioan Lloyd at Bristol and Christ Tshiunza at Exeter Chiefs are also earmarked as players with big futures.

Patience will be required initially, it always is, but there is every reason for Welsh fans to be excited about the future of Welsh rugby. There are an interesting few years ahead.

Team Wales at the 2019 Rugby World Cup

Management Team
Warren Gatland - Head Coach
Rob Howley - Attack Coach
Stephen Jones - Attack Coach
Shaun Edwards - Defence Coach
Robin McBryde - Forwards Coach
Neil Jenkins - Skills Coach
Alan Phillips - Team Manager

Players	
Forwards	**Backs**
Wyn Jones	Gareth Davies
Nicky Smith	Tomos Williams
Rhys Carre	Aled Davies
Ken Owens	Dan Biggar
Elliot Dee	Rhys Patchell
Ryan Elias	Hadleigh Parkes
Tomas Francis	Jonathan Davies
Dillon Lewis	Owen Watkin
Alun Wyn Jones (C)	Josh Adams
Jake Ball	George North
Adam Beard	Owen Lane
Cory Hill	Hallam Amos
Bradley Davies	Liam Williams
Aaron Wainwright	Leigh Halfpenny
Josh Navidi	
Aaron Shingler	
Justin Tipuric	
James Davies	
Ross Moriarty	

Backroom Staff
Paul 'Bobby' Stridgeon - Head of Physical Performance
Huw Bennett - Strength & Conditioning Coach
John Ashby - Strength & Conditioning Coach
Ryan Chambers - Sports Scientist
Jon Williams - Squad Nutritionist
Andre Moore - Team Chef
Rhodri Bown - Head of Analysis
Marc Kinnaird - Analyst
Andrew Hughes - Analyst
Chris Berry - Analyst
Prav Mathema - National Medical Manager
Geoff Davies - National Squad Doctor
Marc 'Carcus' Davies - Senior National Squad Physiotherapist
John Miles - Senior National Squad Physiotherapist
Angela Rickard - Soft Tissue Therapist
Hanlie Fouche - Soft Tissue Therapist
Caroline Morgan - PA to National Squad and Team Management
John 'JR' Rowlands - Baggage Master
Luke Broadley - National Squad Media Manager
Sebastian Barrett - Digital Media Manager
Trystan Jones - WRU TV
Ben Evans - Team Photographer

St David's Press

Nerves of Steele
The Phil Steele Story

'I've been lucky enough to get to know Phil during my time as Wales coach. He is an excellent broadcaster who genuinely wants Wales and Welsh players to excel and I respect his friendly and personal approach. I also admire the fact that he has been able to do this while facing personal and life changing challenges.' **Warren Gatland**

'Phil Steele embodies all that is great about the culture of Welsh rugby. His strength of character and sense of fun are all the more impressive given some of the dark and devastating times he has endured.' **Caroline Hitt**

Known to thousands of rugby fans as a knowledgeable, passionate and witty broadcaster, and as an entertaining and popular after-dinner speaker, Phil Steele's confident demeanour and humorous disposition mask a life-long battle against depression and anxiety heightened by heartbreak and tragedy in his personal life. *Nerves of Steele* is a remarkable story and reveals the real Phil Steele, a man known only by his very closest friends and family.

978-1-902719-50-4   208pp   £13.99   PB
978-1-902719-53-5   £9.99   eBook

2 Hard to Handle
The Autobiography of Mike 'Spikey' Watkins

'One of the most inspirational leaders that Welsh rugby has ever produced' **Mike Ruddock**

'A great friend...also a great inspiration...he led from the front and his team mates could always rely on him when things got a bit rough, even though he'd probably started it!!' **Paul Turner**

'No one trained harder, no one played harder...heart of a lion' **Terry Holmes**

One of the most colourful and controversial characters in Welsh rugby history, Mike 'Spikey' Watkins remains the only player since 1882 to captain Wales on his debut, and win.

978-1-902719-40-5   251pp   £18.99   PB

The Indomitable Frank Whitcombe
How a Genial Giant from Cardiff became a Rugby League Legend in Yorkshire and Australia

'Frank Whitcombe was a rugby league cult hero in the days before there were cult heroes. An eighteen-stone battle tank of a prop forward, he graduated from Welsh rugby union to become a pillar of the great Bradford pack of the 1940s. In the process, he became the first forward to win the Lance Todd Trophy, a member of the 1946 'Indomitable' Lions touring team to Australasia and had even driven the team bus to Wembley when Bradford won the 1947 Challenge Cup Final. This book is his story - it is essential reading for anyone interested in the history of rugby and the amazing men who made the game.' **Prof. Tony Collins**

'Frank Whitcombe became a Welsh international and a Great Britain tourist. He is widely regarded as an all-time great of rugby league.' **Fran Cotton**

978-1-902719-47-4   256pp   £19.99   PB
978-1-902719-59-7   £9.99   eBook

St David's Press

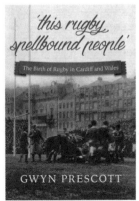

'this rugby spellbound people'
The Birth of Rugby in Cardiff and Wales

'...scrupulously researched [and] well written...Gwyn Prescott has given [rugby in Wales] a history to be proud of.'   **Huw Richards, *scrum.com***

'Prescott paints a meticulous picture of Welsh rugby's growth in Victorian Britain'
Rugby World

'...a fascinating piece of research and a major contribution to the history of rugby.'
Tony Collins

The Birth of Rugby in Cardiff and Wales superbly reveals the importance of rugby in Cardiff and to the significance of Cardiff to the development of Welsh rugby in the nineteenth century.

978-1-902719-43-6   304pp   £16.99   PB

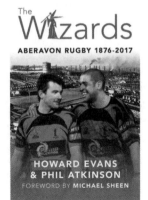

The Wizards
Aberavon Rugby 1876-2017

Howard Evans & Phil Atkinson

'I would rather have played rugby for Wales than Hamlet at the Old Vic. To that town, Aberavon and its rugby team, I pledge my continuing allegiance, until death.'
Richard Burton

One of the traditional powerhouses of Welsh first class rugby, Aberavon RFC has a long, proud and illustrious history, with 50 of its players being capped for Wales, the club winning many league titles and domestic cups, and - with Neath RFC - facing the might of South Africa, Australia and New Zealand. Aberavon RFC is a great rugby club and this is its story.

978-1-902719-66-5   256pp   £19.99   PB

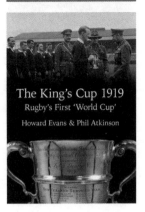

The King's Cup 1919
Rugby's First World Cup

Howard Evans & Phil Atkinson

'An intriguing retelling of a significant but largely forgotten chapter of rugby union history, superbly illustrated.'   **Huw Richards**

'Howard is an authority on rugby's history and meticulous in his research'
Andy Howell, *Western Mail*

After the Armistice in November 1918 – with the forces of the world's rugby-playing nations and many of their stars still stationed in Britain – and with the public desperate to see competitive rugby played again, an inter-military tournament was organised. King George V was so enthused by the proposed competition that he agreed to have the tournament named after him, and so The King's Cup was born.

The King's Cup 1919 is the first book to tell the full story of rugby's first 'World Cup' and is essential reading for all rugby enthusiasts and military historians.

978-1-902719-44-3   192pp   £14.99   PB

ST DAVID'S PRESS

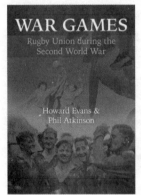

War Games
Rugby Union during the Second World

'The intention behind *War Games* is to provide, for posterity, a record of 'the great game' during the war years, and of thosre embroiled in the conflict who held a deep passion for rugby and sought every opportunity to play the game.'

Phil Atkinson, from his Foreword

Dedicated to 'all those in rugby who did - and who didn't - make it through those troubled times', *War Games* is a comprehensive and highly illustrated commemoration, packed with stories and statistics that for the first time chronicles the history of rugby - the men and the matches, from 'scratch' to international - during the Second World War.

Starting with the short-lived 'infant' season of 1939-40 and ending with the 'Victory' series of internationals in 1945-6, and including the hugely successful New Zealand Expeditionary Force (NZEF) 'Kiwi' tour of 1946, *War Games* details all the major rugby contests and the hundreds of players including: Bleddyn Williams, Prince Alex Obolensky, Bill McLaren, Wilf Wooller, Blair Mayne, Sir Tasker Watkins, Ralph Sampson, Gus Risman, Willie Davies, Les Manfield, Charlie Saxton, Fred Allen and Jim Sherratt.

Essential and entertaining reading for followers of rugby and military historians alike, respected rugby authors Howard Evans and Phil Atkinson tell the tale - meticulously and with great affection for the game they love - of those men who played for fun but who, on too many occasions, lost more than a rugby game.

978-1-902719-67-2   302pp   £25   PB

'Call Them to Remembrance'
The Welsh Rugby Internationals who died in the Great War

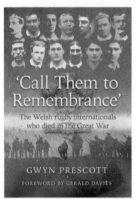

'This book is [an] acknowledgment of the sacrifice made by 13 Welshmen....Theirs was a sacrifice which needs to be told....Gwyn Prescott, with meticulous and sympathetic attention to detail, tells the story. This narrative is an essential record.'   **Gerald Davies**

'These humbling stories describe 13 individual journeys which began on muddy yet familiar Welsh playing fields but ended in the unimaginable brutality of the battles of the First World War.'

www.gwladrugby.com

'This is a book which moves as well as informs, combining impeccable scholarship with deep human sympathy. In recounting the active lives and terrible deaths of the 13 Welsh internationals who died in the First World War Gwyn Prescott not only offers a fitting tribute to their sacrifice but paints a vividly compelling picture of Wales, and the increasingly important role that rugby played in Welsh life, in the decades leading up to 1914.'   **Huw Richards**

'Gwyn's thoroughly-illustrated pages... [goes] fully into the background, detail and human dimension...to splendidly sad effect in typically meticulous and sympathetic fashion'

Touchlines - The Rugby Memorabilia Society

'*Call them to remembrance*', which includes 120 illustrations and maps, tells the stories of thirteen Welsh heroes who shared the common bond of having worn the famous red jersey of the Welsh international rugby team.

978-1-902719-37-5   170pp   £14.99   PB